Helping Dreams Survive

The Story of a Project Involving African-American Families in the Education of Their Children

by
Jocelyn A. Garlington
Foreword by Michelle Fine

published by
National Committee for Citizens in Education
900 2nd Street, NE, Suite 8
Washington, D.C. 20002

Copyright 1991 National Committee for Citizens in Education
Editor: Chrissie Bamber
Design and Illustration: Jerry Prettyman
Photos: Darrell Taylor and NCCE staff

ISBN No.0-934460-38-8
Library of Congress Catalog Number 91-62795

Manufactured and printed in the United States of America.

A Word of Thanks

The National Committee for Citizens in Education gratefully acknowledges the support of the Lilly Endowment, Inc. in the development and publication of this guide.

NCCE also wishes to thank The Prudential Foundation for its operational support of the "With and For Parents" project over a 42-month period, the William G. Baker, Jr. Memorial Fund for supplemental support and assistance with the development and purchase of reference materials for families in the project and the W. T. Grant Foundation for underwriting the project evaluation conducted by the University of Pennsylvania.

About the Author
Jocelyn A. Garlington

Jocelyn Garlington joined the National Committee for Citizens in Education in 1986 as an associate for dropout prevention. That year she was named assistant director of the fledgling "With and For Parents" program in Baltimore, Maryland. In 1989, the long-time Baltimore resident was named director. The project's first director, William Rioux, assumed larger leadership responsibilities that year as NCCE's executive director.

Prior to her association with NCCE, Ms. Garlington worked in the field of Adult Literacy in Baltimore, coordinating the city's literacy services and the literacy volunteers program for the Enoch Pratt Free Library System. She has also taught English in private and public schools.

Acknowledgments

Without Bill Rioux, the project's founder and first director, this book would not have been possible. Dr. Rioux conceived the "With and For Parents" project after conducting extensive research into dropout prevention and working with programs for low-income minority families around the country. This led him to make an out of the ordinary six-year commitment to shattering the myth that low-income Hispanic and African-American parents cannot play a significant role in their children's education.

Numerous people in the Harlem Park community have provided valuable assistance during the writing of this book and over the last four years when the "With and For Parents" program was a fixture in their neighborhood. Reluctantly, I attempt to name a few, knowing I make grave omissions. Without these folks, we on the "With and For Parents" staff would have had a much harder road to travel in settling into the community, in getting to know the school staff and community workers and in learning about the families we hoped would become friends and partners. There are friends of friends to thank and parents of parents and cousins and older brothers and sisters and old friends who no longer live in the neighborhood but continue to hold it dear; and folks who never lived in the community but felt our mission was worthwhile and came to help when they could.

I would like to thank the staff of St. Gregory's Church, Father Damien and Deacon Tom Yorkshire, who welcomed us and were generous with advice, encouragement and the use of church facilities, including the church van to provide transportation for parents. Madeline Pullen, president of the Lafayette Association, deserves a special thank you for introducing us into the network of community organizations, also the 12 members of the "With and For Parents" advisory committee. At the Harlem Park Middle School, Principal Donald Murray and Director of Guidance Geraldine Hooper helped to strengthen our influence and effectiveness among the school staff and students, and Theresa Oseitutu collected student data and helped us with our initial contacts with families. Lawrence Howe and Lynn Leslie of the school district's central office assisted us in procuring and interpreting follow-up data on the students who went on to high school.

I acknowledge and thank parents—too many to list— who in their special way contributed so much to the program and to our understanding of what must be done to involve parents more fully in the schools. A very special acknowledgment is owed to the parent pioneers who brought the "With and For Parents" Club from an idea to a fully functioning parent-run organization in the Harlem Park Middle School: the club's first president, Phyllis Price; vice president, Camilla Montgomery; treasurer, Kathy Talbot; and secretary, Ianthia Darden; also "tried and true" members Barbara Easly, Bertha Moore, and Bernadette Green who were there when we needed them most.

Ethnographers Michelle Fine and Donelda Cook

documented progress in a special way. Their interviews and oral histories of local families chronicled parents' changing outlook about their influence on the school success of their children. Gayle Dorman of the Lilly Endowment, Inc, offered valuable direction and feedback throughout this writing project. Readers whose comments of an early draft were most helpful and led to many improvements in this text are Rev. Norman Handy, William Kerewsky, Donald Murray, Karen E. Kelley, Bryan Samuels, Linda Howard, Anne C. Hallett, and Edward J. Meade, Jr.

My fellow staff members at "With and For Parents," Robert Gregg, Coretha Holly, Joyce Coleman, and Bertha Moore, deserve as much of the credit for this endeavor as I. Also offering valuable assistance were other members of the NCCE staff: Chrissie Bamber, for designing informational materials for parents and for her ongoing editorial assistance through the many transformations of this manuscript; Nancy Berla, project advisor, for keeping issues before us and organizing and interpreting project data, Susan Hall for her careful proofreading and Lisa Mondor for her secretarial and desktop publishing skills.

Finally, to my father, Luther Garlington, thank you for exterminating the bugs (and worse), fixing the locks, chauffeuring us all and being an all-around good guy. You were always there when we needed you.

Jocelyn A. Garlington, Director
"With and For Parents" Program

CONTENTS

Foreword

It seems fashionable these days to say that families and schools are partners in children's education. In the 1990s, low income African-American families appear to be the "disparaged partners." As urban communities deteriorate, these families pay dearly the price of class and race stratification and, in turn, are blamed for their own impoverishment. We hear that the problem with public education is that they don't care. They can't raise children. They are "children having children." And they are robbing us of our international competitive edge.

The volume you are about to read is powerful testimony to the contrary. The text speaks to the strength, persistence, trouble and passions of low-income African-American families who are deeply involved in, worried about and connected to their children's education. This manuscript journeys through the biography of "With and For Parents," a program which sought to work with and empower parents; a program which, over time, transformed itself radically to respond to the needs of a community ravaged by a collapsing economy, surrounding racism and unprecedented federal abandonment of urban districts. This volume stands forcefully as our collective witness to the devastation and the collective struggles of urban, low-income parents/guardians. Across these pages, you will hear their words as they mobilize collectively to do the best they can for their children and communities, exhausted by the uphill battle, searching for any light at the end of the tunnel. As Ms. Darden, a local parent activist interviewed during our research for the program, explained:

There is the idea that Black parents don't care about their students—that's not true. I think they are very concerned. A lot of Blacks do not have an education. They may not have gone to tenth, eleventh or twelfth grade; they dropped out of school; they feel as though the school system may not have done what it should have done for them, so they may say, "I'm going to put my child in that school system, and I'm not going to be bothered. I'm just going to let them teach and that's that." But that is not the way the process should work. I know that if there is to be a better education for my children, I have to be the force, I have to be seen, I have to be heard.

Feeding and feeding, just like you would a child, that is how we need to nurture the parents. And being a parent is not so easy as people think, whether you're Black, whether you're White...it doesn't make any difference. Parents are still growing just as their children are. My mother encouraged us to get an education. I'm 35 and she's still saying to me, "You go back to school and get some more education because education is an ongoing process."

Jocelyn Garlington has narrated a story of parents/guardians who are prepared to be critical activists in social movements for educational and economic justice. No one, any longer, can argue that they are uninterested, incapable of helping, unconcerned. Indeed this volume forces us, as a culture, to face ourselves harshly; to retrieve blame from those families who have paid dearly for the greed and elitism of the U.S. economy; and to ask squarely whether or not we have the political will to work in solidarity with low income families for social justice. With few resources, an unstoppable desire to believe and a collective passion to persist, these parents are asking educators, policy makers and advocates for help. The national response you will hear to them is both undermining to and cynical about their dreams.

The Conservative Right, through the State and private interests, is pressing deep and broad for the privatization of urban schooling. In order to escape racial and class integration, they are advocating "vouchers" and private sector "choice." As we know well from health care and housing, the move to educational privatization is a move to further class and race oppression. But as devastating as the Right, are those who constitute the silenced majority— liberals who are outraged, but sufficiently comfortable to have exited the public schools, moved from communities of violence, retreated from cities of decay and now have given up on the public sector.

Jocelyn Garlington, Coretha Holly, Robert Gregg and Bill Rioux, as well as the parents with whom they have worked, lay a powerful challenge at all our feet. They ask, what are we willing to do with low income parents about the struggles of public education? Will we join them, or will we, too, turn our backs? Once you have read this text, whether educator, policy maker, activist, practitioner, and/or parent, you will acknowledge that if we do turn our backs on these parents, then we will have refused to engage in the struggle for public education. This text needs to fire up all of us toward organizing a broad-based, cross-class and cross-race coalition of educators, parents and activists struggling together for rich, quality public education for all.

I dedicate this to Koray Maddox, our foster child, murdered at age 16, on May 20, 1991. We all need to fight for better. Our children deserve it.

Michelle Fine, Professor
University of Pennsylvania

Preface

This Book: What it Is and What it Is Not

This is not a conventional guidebook. Yet, we hope it will guide those of you who have program responsibility for involving low-income minority families in the education of their children. This book will not lead you step by step through a process nor explain every facet of a "model" program. (There are no claims that the "With and For Parents" program herein described is by any means "model.") You will find no charts, timelines, sample budgets, training models or needs assessment instruments to duplicate and replicate. Yet, this is a guide. And for those who believe that families are the school's true constituents and that they must be in a position of influence and authority if their children are to become fully educated, this may be one of the most important guides you will read.

This is a guide to a particular world. The focus is on the poor, the disadvantaged and the disenfranchised. This is the sub-culture that most people, including school personnel, want, by their behavior and attitudes, to deny exists. These are families who by and large are not enfolded into the educational process, who are seldom understood or listened to by teachers and school administrators and who feel treated more as an annoyance than an asset when they attempt to interact with schools. This is a world in which the blame falls on the victims when institutions fail to meet their needs. Even those who have a commitment to trying to help may not have a basis for rational and sure-footed plans and decisions. This world is complicated, difficult and simultaneously shot-through with weaknesses and disadvantages, yet unexpectedly strong and resilient.

"With and For Parents" lived in this world for four years, the staff shaping its collective professional life and aspirations to become a part of the lives of families. This acceptance and trust was hard earned. Whereas the neighborhood schools were open only on weekdays and with limited summer hours, the staff of "With and For Parents" was available to families year-round, including many evenings and weekends. During the course of the project, we made endless modifications; we did much rethinking and re-evaluating of approaches and of the daily operation, and reexamining possible reasons for successes, failures and reversals.

This book is more than a guide for intervenors; it is a recollection of a long-term experience working with inner-city families without prescriptions or dictates but with energy, creativity and faith. We, the staff of the "With and For Parents" project, hope that what you read here will shed light on that uncertain path leading to success in reaching families who for so long have been ignored or forgotten by schools. There are no quick fixes or magic formulas rendered here. There are no blueprints or rigid guidelines. What you will find is information, suggestions, procedures and cautions that will enable you to be more valued and effective participants in a setting that was previously foreign, misunderstood, and "resistive" to change.

Introduction

In the summer of 1987, the "With and For Parents" program opened its office in a community service center located in the Baltimore, Maryland, neighborhood of Harlem Park. The concept for this project, to increase the influence of low-income minority parents over their children's decision to remain in school until graduation, was developed by William Rioux, executive director of The National Committee for Citizens in Education (NCCE), after an extensive search for dropout prevention programs that significantly involved parents. NCCE, a nonprofit organization long dedicated to improving public schools through increased parent and citizen involvement, has focussed in recent years on the critical educational needs of low-income, minority and urban families. Research has shown consistently that parents of all income levels can have a positive influence in shaping their children's attitudes about school and the value they place on education. Yet, in dropout prevention programs, parents (especially low-income minority parents) seem to be either forgotten or viewed as part of the problem. Believing that these parents need special encouragement and support in order to become active and influential, NCCE designed a project just for them. Measures of the project's success would include establishing a pattern of assertive parent interaction with the school and making a positive difference for their children in terms of achievement, promotion, and continued school attendance.

In late 1985, NCCE approached The Prudential Foundation as a possible sponsor. Prudential agreed to be the primary funder of the project, and a site was chosen in Baltimore after a review of five urban areas.

The National Committee for Citizens in Education made a three-and-one-half year commitment to work closely with a significant number of families of incoming sixth graders at the Harlem Park Middle School through their children's matriculation to high school. One hundred fifty-six families residing within a 10-block area of the school were selected for the experimental group. All were African-American. A "control" group was then selected, matched for race, gender, age, placement and CAT scores of children in the experimental group. The control group would facilitate statistical comparisons to determine the impact of the project. During the three years of the project, data was collected both for the sample group and the control group including attendance, grades, test scores and retentions.

NCCE staff worked collaboratively with the Baltimore City Schools throughout the term of the project. Research and evaluation consultation was provided in the planning stage by Joyce Epstein of Johns Hopkins University. The actual research component of the program was conducted by ethnographic researchers Dr. Michelle Fine, of the University of Pennsylvania, and Dr. Donelda Cook, of the University of Maryland, under a special grant from the W.T. Grant Foundation. Their ethnographic approach to research in the dropout prevention field was highly compatible with the goals of the "With and For Parents" project. From the interviews Fine and Cook conducted with families and the oral histories they compiled, we staff members learned a great deal about parents' personal educational experiences and their deep belief in education as truly the way to a better life—for themselves and their children.

The project staff of five included the director, William Rioux; assistant director, Jocelyn Garlington (later to become director), a Baltimore literacy specialist; parent coordinators Robert Gregg, a retired middle school teacher, and Coretha Holly, a human service paraprofessional and community resident; and secretary Joyce Coleman, a former student at Harlem Park Middle School. Later, Bertha Moore, a mother with a child in the project, assumed the secretarial duties for the project as well as assisting the senior parent coordinator.

During the three-and-one-half years the office was open in the community, we learned much from parents about the barriers that influence their personal level of involvement: years of negative encounters with schools and other public institutions, overwhelming family survival concerns, restrictive employment situations, health problems, difficulties with transportation and child care, and feelings of powerlessness to negotiate acceptable solutions on behalf of their children and loved ones when confronting bureaucracies.

As we review the myriad of conventional and not-so-conventional parental involvement strategies we used, we have a clearer understanding why some work and so many fail. We asked parents to critique our strategies, tell us what to change, tell us what was truly helpful. They did, and we listened. And now it is time to tell the lessons learned from Harlem Park parents.

August 3, 1987

Today, we spent our first full day in the Harlem Park office. Project director Bill Rioux and I spent a lot of time waiting for the phone installer and office equipment to arrive. With no air conditioning, we took turns going out for a bit of air. The space looked so large and empty, like a blank page. We were planning, arranging, forming vivid mental pictures of this bare room filled with people, phones ringing, parents and students coming and going. I went out to the loading platform to "greet" some office furniture. From there I had a clear view of the row houses across the alley. It occurred to me that so many houses I had walked by and paid little attention to in the neighborhood would soon have special meaning. In them lived families I would soon learn to know.

Bill knows I am fond of keeping journals and has suggested that as assistent director I keep one of my experiences with the project, so tonight I have this brand new notebook and a cassette recorder (I will probably never use it) as back-up. Much of what I write will be pure documentation, but I hope to include some worthwhile reflections and day dreams.

September 16, 1987

I drove around the community today at about seven o'clock in the morning. Everything was quiet. I guess few people come out that early on a Saturday morning. I counted twenty-three churches! Steeples were everywhere I looked. I wonder what it was like to live here when the neighborhood was elite? There is still grandeur. My parents tell me this was truly an "elegant community for Negroes." I can look at the houses, even in the shape they are now, and imagine the elegance.

Now, few businesses thrive here, and many of the ones that do are liquor stores. The funeral homes seem to be doing very well. Aside from the churches, they are some of the best maintained properties. Given the times, I suppose business is booming.

The Neighborhood

Exploring Harlem Park

In the heart of West Baltimore's dense residential area, several miles of streets lined with row houses lead back to a rectangular strip of park. On the northern-most tip of this open space sits the Harlem Park Middle School and the adjoining Harlem Park Elementary School. Despite their current states of dilapidation and abandonment, some of these houses have remnants of a former pride of ownership: fragments of imported tiles in the foyers, elaborately carved eaves, impressive turrets and stunning floor-to-ceiling windows which are shattered or boarded up. Lining the streets are a few thin trees struggling to survive in small dirt squares carved in the concrete and covered with steel grates that trap trash and broken glass. Many of the houses have the traditional marble steps found in communities all over Baltimore. Some are kept sparkling white in the tradition of generations of Baltimoreans before, but all around is a pervasive feeling of abandonment.

Walking down streets of what seem almost endless brick and stone houses prompts curiosity about their interiors. On the exterior, many of them seem unlivable. Rows of weather-beaten, vulnerable doors have an eerie quality of sameness. The houses, in various states of ill-repair, seem unsuited to providing safe shelter to older people, children and babies. Yet, families do live in these substandard, unhealthy places that offer minimal protection from the elements or the threat of crime.

On humid summer Baltimore days, doors are open, revealing narrow, pitch-black hallways. Occasionally, a shaft of light forces its way through an open back entrance, leading, in most cases, to an alley. Seldom are screen doors at either entrance to keep out insects, rodents or intruders—landlords don't provide them. A house open and exposed to the street this way seems so vulnerable. But for many people in congested urban slums, these brick and mortar boxes are home, and deprivation of comfort, privacy and security is a way of life.

In the summer months, people sit

outdoors on their front steps to escape the stifling heat inside. Yet, outside too, the air is thick and steamy and, most days, laden with smog. Few houses have air conditioners. An occasional window fan sits precariously on a rotting window sill, running heavily and inefficiently. In the winter, houses are shut up as tightly as possible; gaps are visible in door jambs where the cold rushes in and the heat leaks out. Tenants, of course, pay their own heating bills. Landlords do not feel pressed to insulate the houses and close the cracks in order to make dwellings warmer and less expensive to heat for people barely able to pay their rent.

A Sense of "Community": What Is Left To Build On?

Everywhere is the evidence of flight—first White flight and then Black middle class flight. Older long-time residents of the community remember well Harlem Park when "well-to-do Negroes lived here," and a Harlem Park Sandtown/Winchester address evoked pride. The "well-to-dos," for the most part, have followed their White counterparts into the suburbs or into more affluent urban neighborhoods. Those who remain here live in relative isolation, despite the proximity of the houses. These rows of converted multi-family houses contribute to a feeling of transience in the neighborhood. True, there is considerable mobility in the area, but we were surprised to find that while families did move during the three-and-one-half

years we were there, they tended to remain in the Harlem Park Middle School attendance area. For those who did move out of the community, it was important to them that their children, if at all possible, remained in their original schools.

The current demographics for the Harlem Park area are grim. The external manifestations of urban depression are uncomfortably familiar, especially to those who have lived or worked in low-income, urban communities around the country. Yet, it is impossible to know this community until you have a chance to know its people, not as they are represented through statistics, but as individuals with potential as well as accomplishments to their credit. Behind rows of decaying facades real people live, dream and hope. Not all of the buildings in Harlem Park are decaying, declining structures. Not all of the residents fit a common profile of poverty-stricken inner-city dwellers, living from day to day, from assistance check to assistance check, resigned to their economic plight with little ambition or means to improve their quality of life.

Many people to whom we talked, longstanding residents as well as the relative newcomers to the area, expressed a genuine fondness for this community, despite its problems. They spoke of a need to find better housing—but in this community. A few parents have been lucky enough to move into rehabilitated units. They waited, living in unacceptable places until they found decent housing that would allow them to remain in Harlem Park.

There are pockets of community activism tracing back to the sixties when the Harlem Park community was a model for urban renewal with full citizen input. Government funding then was generously channelled into the area, and there was a feeling of renaissance and hope. It is ironic that now, at a time when this community needs help most, few resources exist. Now, Harlem Park struggles not to be forgotten. Some residents work tirelessly and without any funding to ensure that this community's voice is heard and that at

each other and smile. And though the current times may not invite the openness that existed a few years back, many residents hold dear the memories of when it was safe to be friendlier, more openly social, safe to let down your guard and trust. This is the strength of neighborhoods and the essence of a community. Though there may be considerable erosion of trust due to an increase of Black-on-Black crime and violence, the bond of race, culture and circumstance prevails. That common thread of experience which seems at times wound so tightly it could snap, pulls people back to the

The residents who choose to live in Harlem Park resent being perceived as trapped in an impoverished area. They live here because of family networks, friends and a history that keeps them connected to this community.

least some of its needs are addressed by the elected officials. A powerful neighborhood association meets monthly and manages to have representation from city government and urban service agencies attend each meeting.

The residents who choose to live in Harlem Park resent being perceived as trapped in an impoverished area. They live here because of family networks, friends and a history that keeps them connected to this community. This is not to say that people are satisfied; they would like safer streets, more community resources, better schools. Yet, it is comfortable to live where people greet

belief that indeed there is strength in unity.

Gone are the days when one could run next door and borrow a cup of sugar but, for many people living in Harlem Park, enough shared sense of community remains to keep calling this community home. This is what we knew was there, though not readily visible, when we began our work. After scratching far below the surface of discouraging demographics, appalling crime statistics and boarded-up buildings, we knew we would find deep pockets of community loyalty and even pride. We wanted to build on these to help tip with an education agenda the scales which seemed so heavily weighted with guilt, shame, frustration and sometimes even hopelessness. It did not happen quickly, and there was no magic in our discovery of people working to support whatever sense of community remained and who had the potential for directing their powerful, self-affirming feelings toward a collective effort for change.

We knew Harlem Park had a sense of community, and we set out to find the remaining spirit and enthusiasm for positive change: the citizens who guard their block from drug dealers, the retired auto worker who is a key organizer, an activist mother who runs her own day care service, or a young man determined to help youth stay out of trouble by forming a basketball team. Finding these "street workers" would be key to getting in touch with the

Finding a Place in the Community

The community center in African-American neighborhoods has great potential for bringing schools, parents and other residents together. Harlem Park has a community center, a building which stands out rather conspicuously among the rows of aging houses that surround it. A modern brick and glass structure located on an active corner one block north of the Harlem Park Middle School, The Lafayette Multi-Service Center immediately catches the newcomer's attention. Its modern architecture stands as a symbol of progress and economic mobility.

After several visits and many discussions with the staff, we decided to open the "With and For Parents" office there. At the time, it seemed a perfect

---

Harlem Park has a community center, a building which stands out rather conspicuously among the rows of aging houses that surround it.

---

pulse of community survival activity. Like many African-American communities, Harlem Park has at its core a deep and abiding belief that education is key to the survival of the community. This affirmation came from everyone, young and old.

location; a child care center was alive and thriving—a plus for us, we thought, as there were bound to be many parents in the project who were making use of the day care facility and who would have convenient access to us. We were convinced by the center's director and program coordinator that its programs and services attracted hundreds of community residents, many of whom had children in the Harlem Park Middle School. It was highly recommended to us by the Harlem Park principal as a place Harlem Park Middle School parents frequented for other services. Needless to say, we were greatly encouraged by what seemed to be an excellent opportunity to work closely with existing programs to fortify and promote interest in increased participation in education.

And so we set up shop, full of optimism and confidence that we were working within a lively and community-responsive setting. We arranged open space to be as welcoming and attractive to parents as possible. Our receptionist and parent coordinators were situated in full view of all visitors, and it was agreed that parents visiting the office would become the immediate priority, regardless of the other activities taking place; no parent was to be left to wait or sit unattended. We had been told by parents that waiting at the school for long periods was common. We experienced this firsthand while waiting to see administrators about the

project. Many times we were seen while parents continued to wait. That experience bolstered our commitment to help parents who came to see us and insist on their right to be respected and treated fairly.

Unfortunately, our office in the community center was located on the basement level with no windows to view street activity. Our floor-to-ceiling glass doors led to a concrete wall. A suite of Health Department offices housing the Baltimore City Lead Paint Poisoning Division was adjacent to ours. Most people who came down to the lower level had received a request to do so from the Health Department. There was little walk-in traffic. When people did occasionally walk by and pause, they were lost and looking for the Health Department offices. We were later to learn that the amount of walk-in traffic for the entire Center had been greatly exaggerated by the center staff.

One advantage of the Center was that it was known to everyone in the

area. We did not have to explain what it was or where it was located; however, despite parent familiarity with the Center, very few visited, and project-sponsored meetings held at the Center were poorly attended. We understood that many variables affected meeting attendance; however, we could not ignore increasing evidence that folks in the community tended not to see the Center as a welcoming place and

resources by the Center's staff.

At the Community Center, we encountered many obstacles as virtual outsiders. While the Center's staff spoke of the need for new programs and services for the community, a certain level of suspicion and even resentment of new efforts prevailed, especially when sponsored by out-of-community organizations, funded by private sources.

A year after we moved into the Lafayette Center, we decided to relocate to a converted storefront on a highly visible corner only two blocks from the school.

avoided coming unless for a specific reason; and when they came, they took care of their business quickly and left. Because of the somewhat isolated location of our office in the building, we saw very few folks who did come to the Center. There was little, if any, promotion of our services and

And so we discovered after moving in that the Center was not what it appeared to be, a viable and important resource housing a variety of community improvement and enrichment activities. Many of the impressive programs displayed in the Center's directory were no longer in operation. Some had fall-

en under the budget ax or were not able to sustain themselves through private funding. Literally hundreds of square feet were dead space; the hours of operation were limited and staff minimal. This community-owned facility existed to provide support services for families and youth, and yet there were few programs and barely enough funding to keep the Center's lights on.

"With and For Parents" was different from the other programs housed in the Center in that it was a prototype effort that measured its success largely on its ability to build effective relationships and eventual partnerships with families toward a common goal. Approaching a pressing education concern—dropout prevention—from a family perspective was unusual but, we believed, the only reasonable approach to improve the school lives of youngsters. Yet, lingering in the minds of many people who had worked in the community was the grave doubt that we or anyone could accomplish anything significant in the area of parental involvement with the great majority of "these parents," given their level of education, lifestyles and priorities. We, of course, were determined to prove that significant and effective partnerships can be formed between inner-city Black families and the school, if attempted with sensitivity and the belief that parents have individual strengths and influence, and are capable of using them to support their children in school. Our position was viewed by many as simply naive.

Our experience in the Community Center was not altogether negative.

We have spent considerable time assessing the negatives in order to help the reader understand the potential damage that choosing the wrong location can have on the success of parent outreach. Much of what may be potentially harmful and disabling to an effort in selecting a site is covert and not easily known to the newcomer who may be courted, as we were, and encouraged to locate in a facility that has a surface reputation for being involved in a constructive and viable way in the community. Often that assessment comes from other human service professionals working, but not living, in the area and not from the residents themselves. We now know ways to learn more about the actual functioning and philosophy of agencies and organizations in the early stages of selecting a place in the community. This is vital if a program is to foster collaborative and cooperative relationships with other community services while maintaining strong program identity and independence.

A year after we moved into the Lafayette Center, we decided to relocate to a converted storefront on a highly visible corner a block away from the community Center and only two blocks from the school. The new location allowed us to be far more flexible in our scheduling of office hours. We no longer had to conform to the Center's hours of operation and could see parents late in the evenings and on weekends. Parent and student traffic increased dramatically, both scheduled visits and drop-ins. The "With and For

Parents" sign on the door was intriguing enough for passersby to stop and ask who we were and what type of work we did. The building had been vacant for quite some time, and there was a natural curiosity about the new tenants. Word quickly spread throughout the community that we were an established presence there.

provide them is essential. Getting out and talking more to people around the community, paying close attention to those who said they seldom used the facility even though it was across the street from their homes would have provided a great deal of information and helped us to make an informed choice.

Visiting a Prospective Site

The mistake we made in our initial selection process was in talking only to the Center staff and not to community people who were potential users of the site. We should have made numerous casual visits before signing a lease. Community-owned facilities are often poorly utilized and in deep financial trouble. A new program represents new life to the Center, an opportunity to expand service and increase community use. We were very interested in supporting existing local facilities, and there were some important advantages in being located in and affiliated with a well-known community service establishment. These advantages range from security to accessibility to community leadership and other human service providers working in the area. However, it is important not to be hasty in choosing a site based on superficial and incomplete observations. Brochures and newsletters do not always tell the truth about the viability, visibility, and cooperative spirit of an agency or organization. "Hanging around" and talking to folks who use the services as well as to those who

Some Important Considerations in Selecting A Community Center For A Parental Involvement Project Site

• A well-kept facility located near the school

• A warm and dedicated staff who share a commitment to the importance of community and family involvement in education

• Security, meeting rooms and KITCHEN facilities

• A day care program, GED, literacy programs or other direct family services

• Center-sponsored after-school and summer tutorial, enrichment and recreational activities, and programs for school-aged children available at no cost to users

• Reasonable rent and a large, adequate space in which to operate

• High visibility

• Recommendations from school administrators and teachers who know the Center and how it operates

• Willingness of Center staff to collaborate and help promote community interest in education issues

• Flexibility in the Center's hours of operation to accommodate the project's needs.

Further Considerations

Physical amenities and a convenient location are good things to look for when considering a community site; however, a less comfortable setting may be better suited to reaching out and making contacts with families because of its reputation for service and responsiveness to the community. Accessibility to the community can be measured in ways other than geographical location. We learned that parents were willing to travel a bit farther to a place where they felt welcome. They flatly refused to walk across the street to a place where they did *not* feel welcome. If possible sites in a community are not situated ideally but are perceived by the community as warm and welcoming, they should be considered, even if transportation or safety problems need to be solved.

The Center where we were initially located offered good security, but primarily for the staff (as if they felt the need to protect themselves from the community). A continuous screening process banned many residents from the building. We found, too, that parents did not feel safe walking to and from the Center despite the security within. The building was situated on a busy corner. Groups of men not only huddled there, but also congregated at the side entrance. After dark, their numbers increased.

In order to accommodate the working schedules of parents, it was necessary to hold meetings in the evening, but the crowds of young men gathered around the Center at that hour deterred parents from coming. A substantial number of parents were reluctant to come out in the evenings for any purpose because of concerns over safety. We asked ourselves how we would feel about walking even a couple of blocks after dark with all of the suspicious activity in the area, most of which appeared to be drug-related. Unlike parents, we staff members went from the Center to our cars or to a nearby bus stop and then home—out of the community.

It is a good idea before settling into a location to drive around during the evening to identify the pockets of activity. Some locations within a so-called "bad area" are relatively quieter and safer than others. In addition, different blocks have their own personalities, and it is wise to learn as much as possible about the differences when beginning work in a community. Again, people living in the area are the best source of information. They will gladly point out the "trouble spots" and answer questions about the community's safety concerns—especially the older residents.

Remaining Neutral

We began in the second year of "With and For Parents" to understand better the impact of political turf on community coalition building. We were cautious not to entangle ourselves in alliances and loyalties. As a result, we were able to remain neutral and to be respected by a variety of community leaders who viewed us as a welcomed resource rather than as competition. We further learned the value of persistence. It took quite a while, but in the third year of operation our outreach efforts to community groups, despite early lack of interest or trust on their part, began to pay off. By attending as many community meetings as possible, encouraging parental support of events, offering our resources to any agency finding them useful and keeping the community leadership informed about our work with parents (largely through mailings), we managed to work effectively with a variety of groups who were at odds with one another. As time progressed, we developed more interactive relationships and built some solid and productive collaborations which increased our capacity to address needs of families. In essence, we followed the advice of a savvy, long-time community activist and leader who became a close friend and supporter. "Just keep doing good work," she advised us. "Keep yourself visible, and people will understand and appreciate what you are doing." That is exactly what we did, though in a later phase of the project we became more assertive in our efforts to build community support and collaboration.

Community Churches: How Much Will They Help?

The Harlem Park community abounds with churches; one virtually on every corner, or so it seems, and many in between. Some are tiny converted storefronts which, from outward appearances, seem to be chicken-scratching for their existence. Others, by contrast, are magnificent stone buildings with imposing steeples, huge stained-glass windows, bell towers, quaint parish houses and shaded courtyards. These idyllic edifices offer sharp contrast to the stark concrete realities that surround them. The most magnificent churches in the area are supported largely by out-of-community congregations and appear aloof and detached from the neighborhood that surrounds them. On Sunday mornings, the streets surrounding the churches are lined mostly with the cars of former residents attending church services. Walking through the community on a Sunday morning would give one the impression that things are not so bad here. Families are well-dressed, and the children look happy and secure. Sunday transforms the community. Things are quieter and, on the surface, safer. If only this harmonious, healthy environment could remain after church services have ended and people return to their respective communities.

In the Black community often the minister is a spokesperson. Harlem Park has no less than fifteen churches in the immediate attendance area. We felt this concentration of Black church-

38

es would offer us many strong and influential voices to champion the cause of community and parental involvement in education. It did not turn out quite as we had hoped, though we were able to work very effectively with some ministers.

It would be unfair to characterize the churches in the community as disinterested or unresponsive. Yet, it became clear to us that many of the churches had priorities which were not focussed on the Harlem Park community. Since churches depend largely on volunteers, where they live and what their priorities are heavily determine that church's level of service to the immediate community. This is not to say that churches are not concerned—they are. But as one minister pointed out, the church is but one institution and cannot handle the broad spectrum of problems that plague inner-city communities.

It is important to learn about which services particular churches in the community offer, whom they serve and where they see a parent involvement program fitting into their scheme of things. Taking time to learn about the churches targeted as potential allies is extremely important. Finding out what their missions are, who the key people are, and the areas where the church feels it may provide support and assistance is the best approach. As we look back on our initial approaches to the community churches, it becomes clear that our outreach could have been considerably more organized and assertive. We should have been prepared to talk about collaboration in concrete terms from the onset, not only to pastors who, for the most part, are terribly busy people and must delegate much of the responsibility for community service, but to the presidents of auxiliaries and other church "workers." These people can be most helpful in designing a partnership with parental involvement programs to complement and to expand existing social service programs the churches administer.

Advantages of Spending Time to Cultivate Church Collaborations

• Churches have high visibility in the community.

• Ministers are often the spokespeople for the community and are highly respected

• Churches have excellent meeting facilities and are viewed as safe, neutral zones.

• Church volunteers tend to be highly organized and quite comfortable with meetings and long and short-term planning.

• Churches generally are non-bureaucratic and tend to be flexible and creative.

• Churches are a great resource for recruiting retired educators willing to spend time planning and helping to implement education programs with a community focus.

We were fortunate to find in the early stages of our efforts a pastor of a Roman Catholic Church who welcomed us and became quite involved in our work. We used his church facilities often and had access to meeting space for large and small gatherings and even parent-organized fund raising events. We also had use of the church van to transport parents. Another church in the community worked closely with us to help with drug abuse interventions. A staff development activity sponsored by "With and For Parents" for Harlem Park Middle School teachers was held

in a large Methodist church located directly across the street from the school.

Church collaborations are important for parent involvement programs. It may take time to nurture these relationships, especially if the congregations do not have families whose students attend the schools in the community. Nonetheless, collaborations can and should happen.

Many churches have tutoring programs and welcome participation and cooperation from the school and from parents. There is a resurgence in many African-American communities of the Saturday schools which were popular in the sixties. Many focus on teaching kids about their African-American heritage and culture and are good places to promote parent involvement in the public schools. The settings are non-threatening and appealing to parents because they provide direct service to children, are nearby, and are run by African-Americans. Many of these programs concentrate on esteem-building which helps both parents and kids feel better about themselves and their potential to be successful.

Some churches in the area sponsor soup kitchens and other emergency services that draw local people. Finding those programs and building a working relationship with churches is an excellent way to address the many survival issues facing families while promoting the education agenda.

Negative Influences

Side by side with churches in Harlem Park is a proliferation of bars, taverns and liquor stores. Harlem Park Middle School and the adjoining elementary school are flanked by liquor stores on the north, south, east and west corners, an atmosphere that deeply concerns community activists and parents. Many of these establishments draw kids because of their video games. Some have become havens for kids hooking school or dropouts looking for a way to fill the empty hours. It is disturbing and a bit ironic that the staff of a school that ranks among Baltimore's highest in daily absenteeism, sits by helplessly while kids slip quietly through the cracks, less than a block away.

The Neighborhood: Some Lessons Learned

• *Getting to know a community is hard work. It is important to walk around, to talk to people, to spend time there, and to be willing to put aside stereotypes and deal with people as individuals.*

• *The streets can be dangerous, but mostly after dark. Exercising reasonable caution as you would in any urban neighborhood makes sense. Leaving doors unlocked or valuables unattended is unwise, but it is not nec-essary to walk around the community with purses clutched tightly, keeping an ever-watchful eye out for potential attackers. The people who suffer most from inner-city crime are those who live in the neighborhoods.*

• *Inner-city neighborhoods do have a sense of community, though it is not immediately discernable to the new-comer. Unfortunately, many communities are fragmented due largely to drug activity and deteriorating economics, and community spirit may be confined to isolated pockets. Finding these activities is well worthwhile.*

• *Consult the clergy; in many cases they will be the community leadership or well connected with it. Finding out where meetings are held and attending them are important first steps in getting to know a community. Appearing on agendas increases visibility, and serving on committees helps trust-building. Much of the community activity takes place in church halls.*

• *Senior citizens are a well-spring of knowledge about the neighborhood, its history, and changes it has undergone. Meals on Wheels programs offer an excellent opportunity to meet and establish relationships with some of the most knowledgeable residents.*

CHAPTER II

November 10, 1989

Ms.—— always apologized for her home when I visited. We suspected she was home a lot more often but did not answer the door or her phone. I was lucky to catch her in a receptive mood on several occasions. I was thinking, as she apologized, that nothing that was wrong with her house was her fault. A health inspector would have had a field day in there, but she kept it spotless, even with seven children! It was amazing. Everything was orderly; beautiful plants and the children's pictures were nicely displayed.

We talked about the rotting state of her front door and how impossible it was to keep the place warm. Besides, she lived on a block with constant drug activity almost on her front steps. I told her she needed a better door for safety. She said she had not considered that. I urged her to push her landlord to replace the door and offered her help in doing so. She did it on her own. The next time I saw her she smiled and said, "I did what you told me to. And I got my door replaced. But the landlord raised my rent."

I could not stop thinking what a bastard her landlord was. But I couldn't shake the guilt I felt either.

Homes

Learning More About Family Life

How do you learn more about the configuration of families? Is it truly necessary that time and effort be spent in finding unobtrusive ways of learning about a student's life at home? And how, if at all, do these efforts affect the success of parent involvement programs?

When "With and For Parents" opened its doors in the summer of 1987, we immediately began planning a comprehensive strategy for reaching out to parents. Ever-mindful that we were strangers to the community, we introduced ourselves and our education agenda in such a way as to invite inquiry from families and others providing a broad spectrum of service to the community.

First Contacts

Our initial contacts with families were crucial. First, a letter was sent from the superintendent of schools endorsing our work and encouraging parents to participate. A similar letter from the principal of Harlem Park Middle School followed as did a letter from the project with a one-pager in question-and-answer form explaining who we were. We felt an urgency to follow the written correspondence with a human contact as quickly as possible.

We decided to meet with each family in person. Setting up the meetings required a staff commitment of literally hundreds of hours. (Many of the families had no phones.) These initial contacts had the potential for determining whether or not we would be invited or at least allowed into homes during the course of the project. The home visit was essential if we were to have any chance of staying in close touch with parents and of being kept abreast of important family life concerns affecting the academic success of students in the project.

We had no assurances that we would be welcomed. In fact, we were fairly certain that invitations would occur after several preliminary conversations with parents along with other forms of contact. At that time, we had not yet hired the project's two parent coordinators and were working with a

skeleton staff which included a guidance counselor from the Harlem Park Middle School. She was assisting us in gathering academic data for the students and initiating contacts with parents.

Enlisting the help of the school counselor was an important decision for us. We wanted and needed the knowledge she brought of the kids and the families; however, we were concerned that her involvement in the beginning phase would affect parent perceptions of who we were and who our true constituents were. Looking back, she played an important role in helping to break the ice with new families entering the Harlem Park school and gave her stamp of approval to parents regarding our intended work. These went a long way to clarify our role with families.

Staffing

It was important that the staff of the project represent the racial composition of the community if we were to promote community ownership and encourage trust and confidence in the mission of the project. Harlem Park is nearly one hundred percent Black, and community organizations are staffed almost totally by African-Americans. We sought a similar composition for the "With and for Parents" project staff. In the first year-and-a-half of operation, the project had only one White staff member, the founder and director of the project. His leadership did not appear to be an issue with families and

school personnel. Only the director of the community center where we were initially housed voiced some resentment over the edge he perceived Whites have in procuring funding for programs in minority communities. If true, this inherent injustice further underscores the powerlessness Blacks have over their destiny and the shaping of their communities. Resentment among community leaders is understandable, no matter how worthwhile and important the project may be, when money for community improvement initiatives is granted to outsiders, especially Whites.

The director of "With and for Parents" fully intended to turn over the leadership of the project to an African-American. That happened in the second year of the project when I was promoted from assistant director to director. But there was no collective sigh of relief when the former director left the scene. He was well regarded by the community and staff, and genuinely missed. Parents continued to invite him to community functions and felt his continued participation was important. This led us to believe that the more important issue for families was not race but rather the ability to trust motives and intent.

In addition to the director and myself, the initial staff consisted of a secretary (a woman who had graduated from the Harlem Park Middle School) and two parent coordinators.

We knew the role of the parent coordinators would be key in establishing a project identity with families, and so we selected them carefully. They needed a deep commitment to families and an extensive knowledge of the community. A willingness to learn about how schools operated, and the nuts and bolts of organizing parents around school issues were other qualities we wanted. We interviewed primarily in the community, sending our announcement to community centers, churches, the housing project and the neighborhood schools. One of the coordinators we hired had grown up in the Harlem Park community and had children who had recently graduated from the schools. She closely identified with the families there, having shared many of the same struggles and experiences as the single parents with whom we worked. She was extremely sensitive and thoughtful about the best way to reach out without being intrusive. The other parent coordinator was a retired middle school teacher who had taught at a neighboring school in a community with demographics similar to Harlem Park's. He knew many people in the community including parents who were former students. He brought with him extensive knowledge of the Baltimore schools, especially middle schools, and had a firm belief in the importance of involving parents at this critical level. It was an advantage to have a Black male on staff. Together, our coordinators made an excellent team representing different experiences, and bringing diverse knowledge to the project.

Planning Visits to Homes

With the parent coordinators on board by November of 1987, the staff planned home visits for each of the 156 families in the project. Parents wanted many questions answered before they welcomed us into their homes. They needed to understand fully who we were and, more importantly, why we were there asking so much of them when they knew so little about us. We explained that we were not on the school's payroll, but we were working closely with the school. We explained to parents what type of organization the National Committee for Citizens in Education was, that the program was not connected with a city or state agency or with any aspect of the public assistance system, nor was the program church-affiliated. Many parents did not have experience with a not-for-profit organization such as NCCE and did not fully understand how it functioned and how its program affected their lives. Not being connected with any source that was familiar to parents allowed us on the project staff to begin with a clean slate, without a negative reputation in the community. On the other hand, we were asking for a different type of access to their lives: their homes and their children's school records. We were asking a lot. How could families be sure trusting us was safe?

We took time to be careful observers of families in the community, to learn about their attitudes toward the school, how parents felt about receiving people associated with the school into their homes. The staff was aware of, and sensitive to, the issue of privacy and avoided missteps that could result in turning parents away altogether.

We had frequent staff discussions to develop the best strategy for obtaining access into homes, keeping in mind always the importance of respecting parents' rights and wishes. This meant that sometimes we would move slower than we would have liked, but we felt the payoff would be greater trust and confidence in us down the road.

We recognized the danger of seeming too aggressive when pressing for face-to-face conversations about school and the importance of total family involvement at every level. Being perceived by parents as radical, pushy or intrusive would have greatly hurt our initial efforts to build relationships with families. Yet, we had a real sense of urgency. We learned much later from a parent who became very involved with us that initially she ignored most of what we sent to her home. "But you all were so persistent," she said. "I finally broke down and came to a meeting; I knew you weren't going away."

Though we considered home visits to be the ideal way to meet and talk with families, we knew that each visit must be planned very carefully and must have a specific objective. This was vitally important, especially in the beginning when we were establishing our credibility with families while pushing ahead with a very complicated agenda, one which could not be accomplished without the trust and cooperation of parents. Phone conversations advanced us greatly in our efforts to know parents, but they were not a substitute for face-to-face conversations. We made it an objective to meet with each family in the project and devised a broad range of ways to achieve that goal: calling meetings, visiting homes, introducing program staff to parents at the school, inviting them to the office.

Window Conversations

Impromptu visits were for the purpose of introduction, leaving information about the program or verifying addresses and telephone numbers. These were generally brief and rarely afforded us an invitation into the home. They took place primarily on a stoop (the white marble steps that characterize Baltimore urban row homes) or from an upper story window. We had many window conversations during our four years in Harlem Park, a device commonly used by residents of row houses and apartments both to hold visitors at a distance and to save the time it would take to walk down several flights of stairs to answer the door. We would ring the bell, wait for the person to poke her head out of the window, then announce who we were and why we were there. These conversations could be friendly or off-putting, a "window of opportunity" for getting to know families better or a brick wall blocking communication.

When parents had phones, these visits were set up in advance. The fact that parents expected us did not mean they had made a commitment to welcome us, and they often used the screen door, a window or another family member as a buffer.

When we visited parents without phones, we made it clear that we did not wish to intrude by dropping by unannounced but that it was very important that we meet them, invite them personally to an event, or share with them some important information about school or other matters of interest to them. If we were turned away (and sometimes we were), we left on a positive note, expressing regret that this was not a good time to visit. A truly effective home visit, we discovered, requires mutual consent. Visits cannot be forced regardless of the sense of urgency the program staff member may feel.

Documenting Visits

Through a series of phone calls and window conversations, we did eventually gain entry to the homes of 90 percent of the children in the project. All home visits, attempted or completed, were carefully documented. The parent coordinators used a form which provided at-a-glance information on the visit. It was not our style to take notes while visiting. We wished to avoid the appearance of gathering information to record in some file, possibly for a hidden purpose. We wanted parents to relax, trust us and our motives but, most importantly, to have a clear understanding of why we were sitting in their living rooms. If we needed to jot down a date, a question a parent wanted answered or an important follow-up agreed to by the coordinator and the parent, we did it openly.

Addressing Family Concerns

As families began to share with us intimate details of their lives, our home visits often addressed a variety of concerns that fell outside the education arena. Home visits usually had as their primary objective a pressing school-related concern (attendance and discipline problems most frequently) based on information we had learned from parents and school staff. Solutions to education and family survival problems had to be fully integrated in a successful home visit. The process of finding acceptable solutions to such problems as unemployment or lack of suitable housing often could be a lengthy one. It was important for us to devise a way to keep families involved and confident that solutions were indeed on the horizon during times when some problems seemed to them genuinely overwhelming. Some home visits were for the purpose of reassurance and encouragement; others were for gaining parental consent and cooperation for taking the next important step in an ongoing process.

Well aware that family concerns and priorities were apt to change daily, we frequently reviewed progress toward integrating education issues into daily

We had many window conversations during our first four years in Harlem Park, a device commonly used by residents of row houses and apartments both to hold visitors at a distance and to save the time it would take to walk down several flights of stairs to answer the door.

family life. We understood that the likelihood of education issues rising to the top of the list of priorities was small for families under enormous daily pressure to keep households intact. Frequent contact was essential to ease education into a more prominent position. When parents allowed us into their homes to discuss education matters, it was an important commitment for them. When parents said, "come in," they were in essence saying yes to education as a family matter. It was our responsibility to assist them in sustaining that commitment, while at the same time remaining sensitive and responsive to other pressing family concerns. This responsibility greatly expanded the range of service, advice, referral and assistance parent coordinators offered each family.

Our developing relationships with families were like blossoming friendships; the more we came to know and accept each other, the more we felt compelled to help. Typically, our families experienced multiple hardships which greatly complicated their ability to increase their involvement in their child's school. Because the parent coordinators' time was limited and the needs great, we developed the family inventory as a way of keeping track of family problems and finding partners in the community service network to provide additional family support.

The following are examples of family inventories. They include problems which are not exclusive to poor minority families but which, for families with limited monetary resources and access to outside assistance, can be devastating.

Characteristics of Family "A"

- Mother is "suspected" of not being attentive to her child's welfare.
- Father fights and wins custody.
- Father is suspected of sexually abusing the child now in his custody.
- Student is involved in a car accident with two adult fatalities.
- Student's continuance in special education is up for review.

Goals for Family "A"

- Set up a line of communication between the school, the project, the custodial and non-custodial parent.
- Refer parents and child to counseling to help cope with the accusations of sexual abuse.
- Ensure that the student is well represented at the IEP review and that both parents fully understand the school's recommendations for placement.
- Arrange with parents for the student to participate in the "With and For Parents" peer support group.
- Keep in regular touch with the family to check on student's physical and psychological recovery from car accident.
- Closely monitor student's attendance and watch for excessive absences which may be the result of depression.

Characteristics of Family "B"

• Single mother has five children ages 5-14 with different biological fathers.

• Mother is caring for her sick mother and a grandchild abandoned by her teenage daughter.

• Student in the project has a serious drug abuse problem with glue sniffing (huffing).

• By parent coordinator's observation and by second-hand information, mother may have alcohol problem.

• Student's father is dying of AIDS.

• Biological fathers of other 4 children are not involved with the family in any way, according to the mother.

• Student, according to latest psychological evaluation, has damage to the left hemisphere of the brain which may be the cause of delinquent behavior, poor judgment and anti-social behavior.

Goals for Family "B"

• Develop strategies with parent to help reduce the number of disciplinary removals from school.

• Arrange for assistance to counteract student's increasing involvement in selling and using drugs.

• Work with mother to improve crowded housing situation.

• Help mother get more assistance and cooperation from the school in monitoring student's attendance and cutting behavior.

• Assist mother in finding appropriate counseling for student to help keep temper under control.

• Refer family to help in coping with father's terminal illness.

• Find no-cost supplemental learning and recreation activities for younger siblings while mother works.

• Find emergency baby clothing and furniture for grandchild placed in family's custody.

These goals provided a framework for us to talk with parents about solutions that would free them to think more about the future and the potential it held for themselves and their children. It is important not only to work with families but also to dream with them. Education should be a pathway to dreams, and it is important that someone with whom a family interacts says that and truly believes it. We presented our plans for interventions to parents in the spirit of friends working together to achieve greater things. We would often remind parents that while things looked pretty bad at the moment, their youngsters were in a constant state of change. We asked parents to form a *partnership* with us to make sure that the school made changes that would improve their children's educational development.

Examining Our Perceptions of Home

People who come into communities to do good work often bring with them perceptions based on experiences quite different from the people who live in the community, and expectations that are neither realistic nor fair. Home is shaped by many factors and is most profoundly affected by the condition of poverty. As outsiders entering a community, project staff must take special care to understand fully how people really live and not get caught up in perceptions of how we think they *should* live.

Learning how people live cannot be accomplished with piles of demographic data, surveys, questionnaires or even interviews. Learning about people's lives goes hand and hand with trust-building. Inner-city families have grown weary of being counted, categorized and characterized. This is not to say that substantial learnings about family configurations and homes cannot be gained from surveys designed to increase a family data base. Some surveys sent to families have been successful in producing needed data. In many cases, a number of families will comply with requests to fill out forms, questionnaires and surveys, especially those sent by schools; however, down the road, these clipboard methods of learning more about family life and the home may damage family/school partnerships. This style of information-gathering can undercut the all-important process of trust-building and raise questions in parents' minds about exactly how this information will be used. Many families will cooperate by providing information requested largely because, in many cases, not doing so affects their eligibility for essential services needed for economic survival. There is understandably a high level of mistrust and suspicion among inner-city African-American parents about how information will be used and whether or not divulgence will come back to haunt them.

We asked ourselves, "What do we really need to know about families in order to be effective?" and "How much specific information should we try to obtain about the homes?" Much of the data collected by people working in communities, viewed by them as important and essential, does not affect the success or failure of their efforts. Because we feel we have something good to offer the community and our work may well improve the quality of life there does not give us *carte blanche* to dig around in people's personal lives.

A good way to be shut out of a family's life altogether is to probe in sensitive areas without an invitation. What are sensitive areas? They vary from family to family and are determined essentially by three factors: who is doing the asking, what they want to know, and how the information will be used.

If our goal was to find out whether parents were free to attend meetings during the day, we did not ask questions that related to their employment status such as, "Are you working during the day?" Rather we listed several possible meeting times and asked them to select the one that would be most convenient. Many parents who do work get paid "under the table" to avoid reduction of welfare benefits. To lose this source of income would have a devastating impact on their household. We really did not need to know whether or not parents were employed in order to carry out our function. What we needed to know was when we could talk to them about their children and school. There was no reason to risk alienation by asking too much, too soon.

African-American communities draw a thin line between asking questions that demonstrate genuine concern and a desire to be helpful, and "getting into somebody's business." Needless to say, "getting into someone's business" angers and offends. Low-income Black folks are fairly tolerant and cooperative in supplying information about their personal lives; they are quite familiar with the process for establishing eligibility used by agencies that dole out services or goods; however, they don't like the intrusion into their personal business and would prefer not having to lay bare their lives in order to "qualify" for assistance in obtaining the basics they need to survive. It is a humiliating process that some people must endure throughout their lives.

Living and surviving in economically depressed communities, residents become artful at quickly summing up newcomers and the organizations or institutions these people represent. Generally, everyone is treated politely. But families living in the community are cautious and will supply just enough information to keep themselves eligible for whatever services or "special help" is being offered. They know too well that these opportunities come and go. Dozens of programs have come to the doorsteps of low-income African-American families and yet years later, the quality of life remains the same and, for many, has grown worse, much worse. The steady stream of projects, programs, and initiatives that have poured into Black communities (with few results to which most folks can relate) has helped to chisel away at the hope for a better life through outside interventions. Consequently, we felt that at times we were indulged and listened to politely. We talked about our program and what we wanted to accomplish. We made a three-year commitment to families: we would remain with them through their children's entire middle school experience, and we would be available all year, not just when school was in session. People nodded and said what we were promising was good. But perhaps in hearts hardened by the coming and going of so many "worthwhile" programs, parents might have been saying, "This will probably lead to nothing, but I'll find out more about this program, just in case."

We believed in the strength of families and in the potential of kids. We had to find a way to convey that message even when things looked grim and sometimes hopeless. We were building friendships rooted in reciprocity and mutual respect. We motivated, inspired and learned from each other. A parent commented that she did not know what she would have done if we had not been there to help her through some rough times she was having with her teenage son.

Not all parents and guardians let us into their homes, and some were extremely cautious before finally letting us make a home visit. But only one parent out of the initial group of 156 actually said to us she did not want to be a part of our program, and even she changed her mind a few times. Parents accepted us because they believed, as we did, that there was a great deal of work to be done to improve the quality of education and that it was time for them as parents and influential people in the lives of their children to be consulted, cooperated with, and respected. They believed too that the middle school years are critical times, and they trusted that we believed in the importance and value of parents as partners in the education of their children. They were not certain how this could be accomplished, but at least they were willing to try. No one denied us access to records or complained to the school system about our involvement in their children's education. We were pleasantly surprised by the warm response we received and the long first conversations we had by phone with many parents and especially with grandparents.

What Are the Important Things to Know about Homes?

After much discussion among the staff, we agreed on what constitutes essential information for working effectively with families on school-related issues. We needed to know:

• How many and which adults living in the household share responsibility for the school-aged child or children
• Names and addresses of significant adults and older siblings in the student's life
• Whether or not a grandparent lives in the home
• Whether a responsible older person receives the student when he or she comes home from school
• The adult in the home in whom the student is most likely to confide
• Whether the child lives at the address given to the school, or one or more other addresses
• If there is an arrangement for after-school care and, if so, who is responsible for that care.

Our primary concern was identifying adults who could share in the responsibility of monitoring and participating in the student's school life. The parent coordinators needed to know on whom they could call if parents were not available, to help with interventions, attend meetings and participate (with the permission of parents) in parent/school conferences and events.

We came to know who these people were directly from parents who sometimes brought a relative or a neighbor to meetings, and we welcomed and encouraged their participation.

The above list would be considerably longer if it included things that we wanted to know about families. We settled for the short list because we felt parents would be comfortable giving us that information, and it would be enough to develop working relationships with families around school-related matters. Taking this approach, we actually learned a great deal about family configurations. We came to learn fairly quickly from parents who the people were in the household who would be most likely to take charge in a crisis. We were careful not to ignore a parent and consult another adult who perhaps showed a greater interest; however, we tried to stay in touch with all of the adults in the household who expressed interest in the educational lives of the children in the family.

We lived with several realities about homes:

• We may never get to know all of the important and influential adults in a student's life, especially those who live outside the home and community.

• There may be changes in the configuration of the family that we are not told about, and this may mean reversals in our efforts to keep in close contact with the family.

• Changing relationships in the home may prompt parents to become more distant and guarded about letting us into their homes.

• Personal life crises may prevent parents from reaching out to us—depression or feelings of being overwhelmed may cause parents to become isolated. They may never share this with us but simply become unavailable to us and the school.

• As much as we learned from families, we knew that there were some things they would never confide. Parents defined the parameters of access. Since we were committed to families, we respected those parameters and did what we could for the student without treading on the parent's turf and destroying a fragile partnership.

Examining Our Perceptions of Low-Income African-American Homes: Assumptions versus Realities

An expanded perception of what constitutes "home" in inner city African-American communities is fundamental. Gathering of specific knowledge about the homes is, at best, gradual.

So often single parent households, female-headed households, are mistakenly labelled "broken" homes. This implies that a former, more complete structure has been fractured and what remains is not only less than it was originally but also less desirable. Many erroneous conclusions are too hastily drawn about the configuration of the single parent home that upon closer scrutiny and a willingness to shake stereotypes and preconceptions can be easily dispelled.

Here are a few examples of assumptions that can block understanding:

Assumption

In the overwhelming majority of cases, no significant male exists in the Black single parent, female-headed household.

Reality

While initially in many of the female-headed homes we encountered no male presence, we found later an influential male either living in the home or living outside of the home but very closely connected with the family. This led us to understand that the male may be invisible only to the outsider.

Assumption

Most single mothers in low-income Black communities don't work, they receive public assistance and are in the home during the day; therefore, they should be available and willing to come to the school for meetings and teacher conferences that are scheduled in the daytime.

Reality

Many single mothers work; some work two jobs and have responsibility

for several children as well. For many, in order to keep public assistance benefits, they must keep their jobs a secret. These jobs are usually very low paying and offer no flexibility in scheduling.

Assumption

In homes where several adults are living, family structure is loosely defined, producing chaos and confusion for the children. These living arrangements are precipitated by economics primarily, and not by the support and comfort provided by an extended family living under one roof.

Reality

African-Americans have a long-standing tradition of extended family living. This does not mean economic necessity does not affect living arrangements significantly; it does. But extended family structures also provide cohesiveness, mutual support and a deep-rooted sense of responsibility for "one's own." Many homes function quite effectively with several adults and their children living collectively and cooperatively under one roof. It is a mistake to judge these homes by the standard White, European-American home composed of a mother, a father and children living as a single unit. Far more productive and useful to parent involvement initiatives is to examine and respect the strengths of various family configurations and to convey to families a desire to know and better understand them.

We tried at all times to convey to parents our respect and understanding of their need to be private and protective when it comes to their homes. If we were turned away or an appointment was not kept or suddenly cancelled, we tried to examine collectively as a staff the possible reasons for that home visit not working out. We looked as closely at our approach as we did parents' reasons for not being available. Were we being pushy or aggressive—to the point of being intrusive? Were we somehow cornering parents into saying yes to a home visit when they really did not want one? Were we plowing ahead with our project priorities and not paying close enough attention to parent needs and responses? Were we assisting parents in establishing education as a priority in the home or were we insisting that they establish education as a priority?

Why Families Keep Their Homes Private and Inaccessible

Crime in the urban community touches everyone. Drug activities have escalated the incidence of Black-on-Black, intra-community criminal activity. It is not uncommon, we learned from talking with parents, to have someone come under some seemingly innocent pretext and "stake out" the home. Later that person, or someone with whom information about your home and its contents has been shared, will return and burglarize it. It may sound paranoid, but we know from talking with several families that it happens often enough to be viewed as a serious threat and as an inevitable occurrence if you "let just anyone into your home." Recently, in a Baltimore housing project, a young boy was brutally murdered by a neighborhood man who only a couple of days before helped the boy's mother carry a school desk into their apartment. The man returned to the home while the mother was at work, and molested and murdered her son. With the rise in the use of mood-altering drugs such as PCP and crack in the Black community has come more brutal and pointless crime, much of it aimed at children and young adults.

Staying out of people's homes means staying out of their business. People in inner-city communities are cautious about others knowing too much about their personal lives. If your neighbor is engaged in illegal activity, it is better not to know about it or to behave in such a way that demonstrates your lack of knowledge or interest in that activity. This is a way to survive, to keep your family safe from reprisal, threats or indirect involvement. The less people know about you and the less you know about them, the better. It is indeed the only reasonable way to survive in an environment where illegal activity provides much-needed income.

58

The physical condition of homes may cause embarrassment. Many families are uncomfortable about receiving visitors because of the conditions of their homes. For many families, the properties they rent and call home are in deplorable condition. Efforts to make substandard housing comfortable are often futile. Water damage, rats, poor insulation, peeling and cracking walls are commonplace. Many parents expressed frustration about trying to find decent housing. Very few low-income housing opportunities are available around the community and those that are have waiting lists averaging five years or longer. We encountered many parents who were embarrassed about the condition of their homes and asked that we meet someplace else. On several occasions parents said to us, "My home is not fixed up the way I would like it." Again, parents want to avoid a situation where they will be judged negatively. They feel that old furnishings, clutter or crowded conditions will send a message that they are incapable of maintaining a "proper" household. They hold off people who might be critical or judgmental so that they will not feel ashamed of their circumstances. People who are shocked when they enter low-income homes for the first time don't have to say a word; their body language says it all. Families feel it and are deeply affected. It is hurtful to low-income parents that their economic constraints prevent them from providing the kind of home they want for themselves and their children. To watch a person recoil upon entering

their home is both humiliating and insulting. Once a family has this experience, they may shut the door to all "outsiders."

Reasons for Discretion in Telling Who Lives in the Home

There are important reasons for being discreet about who actually lives in the home—legal and personal. For some families, it is important that the actual number of people living in the home not become known. There are several reasons for being secretive: Some families have allowed other family members to move in in violation of the lease; sensitive custody issues require discretion about living arrangements; or disclosure could jeopardize a family's entitlement to public assistance.

In the initial trust-building phase of our effort, it was important that families were clear about the role our organization played in the network of social services with which they were most familiar and had some interaction. Parents wanted to know, before letting us anywhere near their homes or into their lives, that confidences would not be betrayed and that information that could result in legal actions would not be shared with other agencies and institutions. We were not reporters of abuses of the welfare system or failures to comply with eligibility requirements. This was not our role, and we were careful even in our in-house record-keeping not to maintain data which might send a red flag to parents that we were somehow in a position to hamper their access to programs and resources. If, for example, a parent chose to use a friend's or relative's address in the community that would make her child eligible for certain con-

of the home or report a loved one to the police because of emotional or economic consequences.

Often younger mothers find themselves feeling helpless to control male adolescents who have ventured into illegal activities. It is equally problem-

---

People in inner-city communities are cautious about others knowing too much about their personal lives. If your neighbor is engaged in illegal activity, it is better not to know about it.

---

siderations, we did not share that information. We were more interested in the parent having access to us and trusting us enough to share the truth about a student's actual living arrangements. Soon the word got out that we were people who could be trusted.

Sometimes illegal activity in the home is suspected or known. In some cases, parents confided that a person in their home was participating in some type of illegal activity. It could be a teenager selling drugs or acting as a drug runner, or it could be that the family bought "hot" goods or a member of the household sold merchandise of questionable origin. The family did not necessarily condone this behavior, though it may have been tolerated because of economic hardship. Usually, it was more a case of a frustrated parent needing help to stop the illegal or undesirable activity. She may have been unable or unwilling to pursue the legal channels necessary. She may not have been able to put the person out

atic to control the activities of grown children, lovers or spouses. All of these situations are complicated and difficult to resolve. Parents, in an effort to ensure that no witnesses see the turmoil of their daily family situations, will simply close their homes to visitors.

Over a period of time, we found that many parents needed someone in whom to confide and were genuinely concerned about the possible consequences of illegal activity in the home for all concerned. They acknowledged a certain complicity by not being more forceful, yet it was clear that there were no easy solutions.

All parents want to do what they can to keep their loved ones from colliding with the law. Incarceration of Black males is so prevalent in this community that most people consider themselves fortunate if a male family member escapes going to jail. Taking steps that would lead to the incarceration of a loved one is an agonizing choice for African-American families. They are understandably protective and will, by necessity, shut the door and work within the family structure to try and get through the dilemma. Doing what is "right" may too often mean betraying a loved one and totally shattering relationships and the home. It is one among many tough choices parents make on a daily basis. Grandmothers, mothers, sisters, brothers, fathers and sons struggle to offset the pain of pervasive crime in their lives. Drugs have changed the community and left in their wake many suffering, innocent bystanders.

We saw this time and time again and tried whenever possible to be friends, not judges. We respected the need for privacy while at the same time keeping in close touch. We were there to help ensure that the school-aged children in the family were receiving an education on which they could build a future. Parents respected and appreciated our mission and allowed us into their lives and their homes as much as possible, given their particular set of circumstances. When going into the home was not feasible, we used other means to keep a line of communication open.

Sometimes people must avoid the bill collector, summons server, social worker and others. Poor folks are virtually besieged by "visitors." It is as though by virtue of being poor, citizens have somehow forfeited their right to conduct their private lives. Bill collectors, rent collectors, insurance salesmen, landlords, summons servers, the police, investigators, social workers, building inspectors, census takers are likely to drop by at some point—mostly unannounced.

It is not uncommon for an investigator or other person looking for a resident on the block in poorer neighborhoods literally to go door-to-door asking neighbors about a person's whereabouts and even questions about his or her habits. This blatant disrespect has made Black folks in the inner-city extremely cautious about even acknowledging that they are home, much less opening the door or even a window to the unannounced visitor. If you are lucky, you may get a window conversation conducted from an upper floor that can vary in mood and length.

Uneasiness may grow when explaining relationships of the adults living in the home. In some cases where adults are living together as a couple, ambiguity or complexity about the nature of the relationship may cause awkwardness in introductions. Parents sense when they are being judged in some way by teachers or other human service professionals. A mother should not be put in a position of explaining the relationship. Though she may simply introduce this male person casually as a friend, the uneasiness and tension remain. If a parent has been made to feel uncomfortable in her own home, it is unlikely she will allow another visit from anyone associated with the school or any other agency if she can possibly avoid it. Many parents of middle schoolers are young (in their twenties) and in a state of flux in their personal relationships. One parent who insisted on coming to us rather than allowing us to visit her confided that she had not attended church since the birth of her children because they were born out of wedlock. She felt people looked down on her and consequently tried to avoid any situation where she sensed she was under moral scrutiny. This woman was a caring parent who desperately needed help for her drug-involved son. She felt terribly isolated and alone, and lacked the confidence to reach out for help. We met her more than half way. Though we never went into her home, we talked with her frequently on the phone and gave her rides to our office. With our assistance, her drug-addicted son was enrolled in a successful recovery program and later placed in an advanced high school curriculum.

Home offers protection from an increasingly hostile and dangerous environment. In low-income urban communities, few places offer family entertainment in a relaxed and wholesome setting. The recreation centers for youth are plagued with violence and drug activity. Additionally, hefty budget cutbacks have caused drastic reductions in staff and the closing of some centers, and have severely hampered sports and other activities for youth and their families. Most parents agree that being on the streets after dark is dangerous—for both the young and old.

In warm weather, the street activity bustles in Harlem Park, and incidents of violence increase dramatically. It is a special challenge in the summer for parents to allow their children to play while at the same time guarding their safety. Many children are required to stay in the house or the yard (if there is one) and are allowed very little freedom to roam or explore. Some parents worry that keeping children so close can actually heighten the allure of the streets, but they see no alternative. Home is viewed as the only safety zone. Families are naturally protective of that space and try to keep as much control as possible over who enters.

Given this mind-set, it is remarkable that families opened their doors to us at all. We were virtual strangers pressing them to take immediate action in an arena they found intimidating and impossible to penetrate or understand. Yet families did accept us.

We attribute much of our initial success in having parents listen to us and allow us in their homes to the fact that we had an education agenda. Education is extremely important in the African-American culture and tradition. Sadly, the quality of education for African-Americans has eroded to the point where families cannot see the direct correlation between education and a productive, fulfilling career for themselves or their children. Kids look around their communities and see adults with high school diplomas struggling to make it. The young drug dealers and their cohorts seem to be doing well, the liquor stores are thriving, lottery sales are booming, but for most of the community, prospects are bleak.

∽

Homes: Some Lessons Learned

• *The long waiting period for decent housing and other related service makes it difficult for parents to see a relationship between action and positive change.*

• *Inner-city homes are vulnerable to crime; they are easy targets for burglary; many families are robbed routinely. Parents cannot be expected to leave their houses unattended for long periods of time. This must be taken into account when asking parents to leave their homes. They have a genuine fear of being burglarized.*

• *Allowing someone into your home is a major decision for many families who live in virtual isolation to ensure they will not become associated with the criminal and violent activity that surrounds them. "Seeing too much can be dangerous"; therefore, parents may be reluctant to discuss what happens in their neighborhood, though the information would be useful in better understanding a student's life outside of school. Wait for parents to volunteer important information about the neighborhood.*

• *There are many configurations of the African-American extended family. Cousins, aunts, grandparents, friends may play an important role in a child's education. Finding the influential person in a home, the one with primary responsibility for raising the school-aged children, is essential.*

• *Home visits are one of the most effective ways to have meaningful conversations with families about school. They can also be some of the toughest contacts to negotiate. Parents must be able to control when home visits happen. They cannot be forced. "Spontaneous" visits can happen only when there is a spoken agreement that it is all right to "drop by."*

CHAPTER III

December 16, 1989

One parent stays on my mind. She is quiet, diminutive, and very pretty. She comes to meetings on occasion, sits alone and sometimes almost seems to disappear. When I talked to her last night, I found a new person. She had been listening to everything very carefully and came over to me after the meeting. She had put a lot of thought into shaping her plan to become more involved. Both of her children were doing well in school, but she recognized her need to become more involved in their school life and learn as much as she could about how the school worked. I did not feel as though I was talking to a shy, compliant person any longer. She is becoming quietly more determined and self-assured, with hardly anyone even noticing.

Parents

Broadening the Definition of Parent

"In Case Of Emergency"

Schools, in an effort to keep current, important information about students' homes, have emergency cards. These index cards are sent home with students to parents each September to be filled out and returned to the school. This is an extremely important document for the school because it provides essential information about the parent's current address. It ensures that the parent or custodial guardian for the student can be easily contacted in case of an emergency. But that tiny card really provides little information about parents, as we were soon to find out in our first attempt to gather basic information about the families in Harlem Park with whom we would be working.

As far as we knew, no other document was designed to gather basic parent/family information. It would be helpful to know, for example, who actually does the parenting of the student in the household. Who would be most likely to visit the school for a casual chat with teachers, bring a student's gym gear or forgotten lunch, or simply visit the school to see what it is like? Who in the family is the person who spends the most time with the student, knows the student best and asserts the greatest influence on the student? These are but a few considerations in determining who has actually assumed the parent role and has ultimate authority in the home. Many times it is not the biological mother or father. In some cases, it is an older brother or sister, people too often overlooked when schools are identifying significant adults in a child's life. Finding out who these people are was one of the first steps for us toward making meaningful contacts with families that result in increased involvement and interaction with the school.

Most parents we talked to over the three-and-one-half years of the project

were quite open about who in the home their middle school student viewed as the person most accessible to them and on whom they relied a great deal. This turned out to be especially true for mothers who were living with their mothers or other older relatives. These mothers in many cases had their children while in their teens and relied heavily on older female fam-

and often almost entirely assumed by the head of the household, most frequently the grandmother. Parenting roles grow and change as the circumstances of the family change; for example, a teen mother may take almost sole responsibility for her child during the early years. (This is not to say that she would not receive considerable support and guidance from her mother

In the families we encountered, most mothers seemed quite comfortable and grateful for the grandmother or others who assisted in raising the children.

ily members and friends to share the difficult responsibility of raising a child at a young age with meager monetary resources.

The Role of the Grandmother

In many African-American homes, the surrogate parent is the grandmother. In some cases it can be an aunt, a cousin or other female relative. In the families we encountered, most mothers seemed quite comfortable and grateful for the grandmother or others who assisted in raising the children. They responded enthusiastically to our request to contact that person directly about school-related matters.

In inner-city families, where teen pregnancy is common, family members band together and take responsibility for caring for the new child. The child is, in essence, adopted by the extended family, and parenting roles are shared

or other family members, but rather that she is responsible for clinic visits and daily care and would be the person most visible in the parenting role.) The young mother often can be seen pushing a stroller and walking young children around the neighborhood. As the child grows older, begins school or enters day care, one sees an increasing visibility of a grandmother or other relative taking responsibility for the child's welfare.

Why? As a child's needs become more external to the home and extend beyond physical care and feeding, the need for greater savvy about institutions, resources and the community arises. Grandmothers tend to take a leading role at this point. Also, by that time, the mother may have another young child to care for and is very much tied to the home with those responsibilities. Additionally, as the children grow older, the mother may tling for a number of parents, especially low-level readers, writing can be even more intimidating. Many parents expressed uncertainty about their writing skills. We tried to assure them this is an insecurity many of us share. Many things contribute to parents' anxiety over writing: uncertainty about grammar, poor spelling, concerns about penmanship. If parents had to write a note to the school, they were particularly nervous. They felt like a student again when everything put to paper is graded.

We avoided creating occasions that would put pressure on parents to write. When a situation did arise that required a letter from a parent, we offered to assist in composing, typing and copying it. This put the weight of the exact wording and construction of the letter on us and took it off the parent. The parent made it clear to us what she wanted to say and was in full agreement with the final draft. She left our office feeling ownership of the document. From that point on, the letter was her letter, not something we composed for her. Parents enjoyed the power of putting their concerns to paper, typed, and well-organized, punctuated with the power of their signature. We always provided copies for parents to keep in their records. Assisting with these letters was among the most empowering activities we initiated with parents. It offered them an opportunity to produce something that might change things for the better. Sadly, for many parents living in poverty, these opportunities are rare. As one

parent told us, "Their whole attitude changed when they saw I had this piece of paper. I told her I was a 'With Parents' parent (I know I didn't say it right, but anyway she knew what I was talking about.) She asked me to sit down and she would be right back. It was the quickest she had ever gotten back to me—and just as nice as she could be. Having that piece of paper really made a difference."

The Case of the Friendly, Disappearing Parent

Much of the work we did with parents revolved around resolving a crisis. Though we talked with parents and provided materials to assist them with monitoring their children's school life and other prevention strategies, we were more likely to see a parent and be able to work with her intensely when a crisis arose. After the problem was solved, we would have far less contact. Sometimes, the parent would be more difficult to reach than before the crisis intervention took place. This we could not understand. Parents told us repeatedly how they appreciated our assistance and how important it was to them to have us there to help. We decided to take a closer look at the reasons some parents with whom we had hoped to have a close association throughout the duration of the project, slipped away. We concluded:

• Solving a crisis at school for many

parents is their way of being involved; to "be there" when they are needed is their perception of parental involvement.

• Parents who have several children find it necessary to center their attention on the one child who needs the most care at a given time. Many families have children living in the home who have severe emotional or physical handicaps that demand a great deal of attention. Ongoing monitoring and home support activities for education take a back seat to more pressing issues.

• Parents need to feel satisfied that they have accomplished something toward improving their child's situation at school. Parents do what they can for their children at the school, and then must turn their energy back to pressing survival concerns in the home.

• While parents enjoyed having us available as a resource, at times they needed a break from our pushing education as a daily priority. During those times, they tended to avoid us.

For years parents had operated on the premise with schools that "no news was good news." Even poor grades in the primary years were not a cause for great alarm for many parents because the long-range impact of poor achievement was not explained to them. Indeed, they were concerned but not informed well enough to be proactive and more effectively involved. And then we came along, five, six, seven years later with a mission to make parents partners in education. We came to them with more information than they had ever had presented to them before. And we brought a sense of urgency, asking them to change the way they viewed their role in education. For some parents it was exciting and something they were willing to try. For others, it was difficult, perhaps a bit overwhelming, and they felt they just could not do all that we suggested. They kept themselves at a distance and, in some cases, were totally inaccessible. Parents were always cordial and many times made commitments they could not keep. This led us to believe they would do all the things that were needed, if only they could.

The "Unreachable" Parent

Despite numerous attempts by the parent coordinators to make contact, about 20 percent of the families in the project remained virtually inaccessible to us. Six months into the implementation phase we conducted an in-depth review of our progress toward the objective of making at least one face-to-face contact with each parent or significant adult in the lives of the students. In some cases, we had made several personal contacts with families through home visits, school introductions, project-sponsored gatherings and chance encounters. We were greatly encouraged by the ease and frequency of our contacts with several families; even contacting parents without phones was progressing nicely. But from some families we could not evoke a response of any kind: Our calls were never returned; home visits could not be negotiated; mail and calling cards were ignored.

A year-end review of academic progress revealed that many of the students on our academic "worry" list were indeed children of the "unreachable" families. This finding caused us to intensify our efforts to contact these families and to have some meaningful dialogue about critical school issues. We had been warned prior to moving into the community that there would be a substantial number (in the school's estimation as high as 75 percent) of parents who would be unreachable for reasons ranging from work schedules to substance abuse. Some, we were told, would remain isolated and insistent on "keeping to themselves." Others simply did not care. We were determined to disprove that assessment and forged on in pursuit of parents who seemed at times as determined to ignore us as we were to make contact. Finally, around the end of the second year, only thirteen families remained with whom we had not made meaningful contacts. Over the next few months, through sheer determination and stubbornness, the number was reduced to zero! Despite that achievement, we did not feel like throwing confetti. While we had finally caught up with these families, no lasting connection was made. They remained inaccessible, never called on us for help, never gave us any encouragement that they might finally become engaged in the project.

This situation created quite a dilemma for us. What should we do about the kids who were in deep academic trouble? Proceed on our own, monitoring and scheduling frequent conferences with teachers without the participation or consent of parents? Could we, in good conscience, write off families? We finally decided that pursuing families who would not meet us halfway was draining valuable staff time and energy that would be better spent with parents who wanted to work with us toward positive solutions for kids. We continued to do what we could for the students of unreachable families and tried as best we could to keep their parents informed, but we accepted the fact that we could do little to change the level of their involvement. It was a tough and painful decision, and we sometimes found ourselves slipping back into old patterns, hoping a contact might be a turning point for a family or student.

∽

Parents: Some Lessons Learned

• *Parents and even grandmothers often appear to be much younger than their age. And some, in fact, are much younger than society's "standards." The younger parent needs to be respected and treated as a person who has authority and the ability to make the best choices for her child.*

• *Many inner-city parents receive little positive reinforcement in their roles as parents and heads of households. More often they are criticized for not doing enough or doing all of the "wrong" things when it comes to their children's education.*

• *While some parents would like to upgrade their education and become better trained for employment, they do not want it to become a central issue. They must be allowed to operate on their own timetable without being prodded or made to feel guilty about not being more assertive in pursuing education and training opportunities.*

• *Writing is uncomfortable for parents who are not illiterate but who feel as though their skills are unsatisfactory. Intervention situations that involve writing may turn parents away from meetings or workshops.*

• *Parents with substance abuse problems must be invited and encouraged to participate. Often they require special attention to help counter low self-esteem associated with substance abuse.*

• *We found it extremely important to remember to ask parents about family members, especially if someone in the family was experiencing hardship. This courtesy affirms for parents that they are being treated as individuals. Remembering names of family members is key to building relationships.*

CHAPTER IV

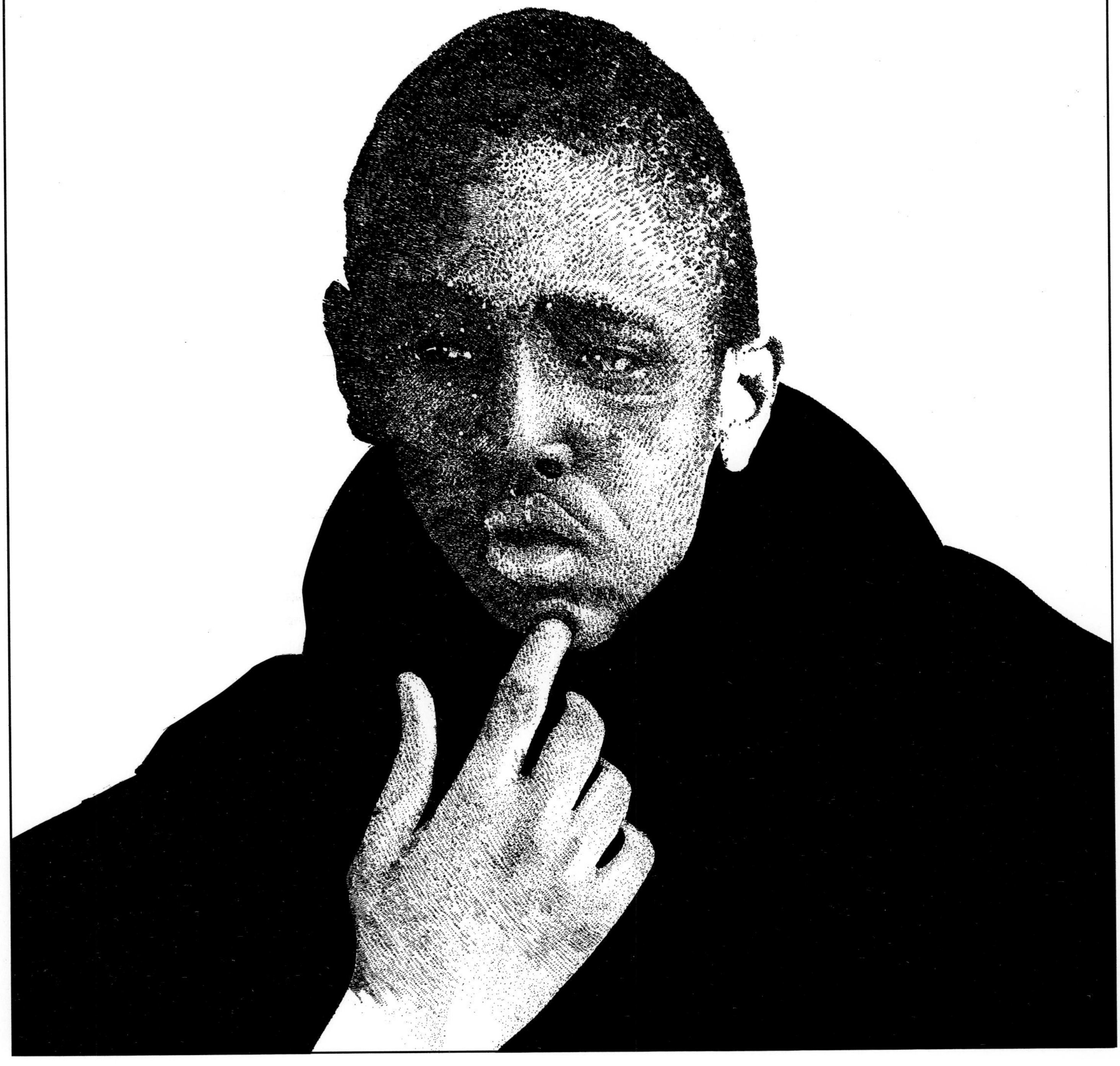

August 15, 1989

When I got out of my car this morning, I noticed Robert, our parent coordinator, crossing the street. He and I must have had the same thought when we went home last night. Even though the agreed upon time for staff to arrive at the office to greet kids and parents for today's trip was eight o'clock, it occurred to us both that at least one student might arrive much earlier. Some days his mother leaves for work as early at 5:30 a.m., and because she is on call, there is no way of knowing in advance when she will leave at that hour.

"What are you doing here so early?" We both knew the answer. And sure enough, before we even had time to put the key in the door, our young friend was turning the corner, carrying his lunch in one bag and swim gear in another. The three of us stood outside the office for a while to catch some of the cooler morning air. Suddenly, it began to drizzle and we went inside. Later, other kids arrived, some gathering inside the office while others clustered in the doorway, watching the rain. Slowly, the office filled with parents and excited kids. I went out to purchase ice and, by the time I returned, the bus had arrived. Robert was on the phone tracking down latecomers. Spirits seemed undamped by the rain. As I waved good-bye to the bus, the sun was beginning to break through the clouds.

to understand that we were not part of the school staff, and it did not take them long to realize that we were indeed an alternative when they needed a sympathetic ear.

Good Neighbors

Our office was arranged to accommodate student visitors. A comfortable loveseat and coffee table filled a loft space providing privacy and a warm, receptive place where kids felt welcomed in much the same fashion as their parents did. We kept soft drinks and snacks for students who dropped by and magazines we knew they would enjoy reading. On the walls were framed pictures of children and parents in the project taken by a professional photographer. Students came in just to show these photographs to friends. The display made students feel important. We called them sweet names, admired a haircut or style of clothing we knew they were proud of. We walked or drove them home when there were concerns about safety and made certain they called home to let someone know where they were and to find out what time they were expected.

We became a friendly neighbor who looked after the kids and took a genuine interest in their welfare. We kept ourselves visible. On hot summer days when the failing air conditioners made it difficult for us to remain inside, we found ourselves stepping out for some relief like the rest of the community, watching people walk by, waving and exchanging greetings. These days were perfect for spontaneous chats with students on their way home from summer school or on a walk around the community with family members and friends.

The staff made every effort to attend as many community events as possible to increase our accessibility to families outside of the office and school, especially those events that brought families together. It was a roll of the dice whether or not we would actually see "With and For Parents" families at these events, but the investment of time was worthwhile. When students saw us in the community outside of business hours, they viewed us not as office workers, but as people who enjoyed the community, and who knew and respected adults and kids in the neighborhood. We might show up at a block party, a special church service, a community festival, school play, sports event, or an anti-drug rally. The high visibility of the project staff and a high level of interaction with the community went a long way toward building trust and gaining the respect of students.

∽

Students: Some Lessons Learned

• *Students can be an important asset to a parent involvement program, especially if an effort is made to invite them to join in activities. It is important to extend personal invitations to students to attend.*

• *An open door policy encourages visits from students. Many students need an adult to talk to—someone other than their parents. It is important that kids know a place they can go when they need help or just want to talk.*

• *Students take pride in their knowledge about how the school operates and enjoy being consulted. They should be given the information their parents receive about school policy and practice, better understanding of report cards, ways to avoid problems at school, explanations of curriculum and grade level expectations.*

• *Most students are willing to talk about grades and academic performance with someone who will listen and not criticize. Students should be invited to discuss grades and other school-related matters in a casual, informal setting—with friends and family members, if they choose. This is a good way to encourage discussion among family members.*

• *No matter how outwardly indifferent kids seem when it comes to adults, most enjoy feeling cared for, needed and respected by adults in their lives. Make students aware that their struggles and triumphs are not going unnoticed and that you are there for them as well as for their parents.*

CHAPTER V

September 23, 1988

It was a very disappointing day. We worked so hard to get our new place into shape for the open house. Not one parent showed up! We could not believe it. We kept watching the door, hoping for the bell to ring.

When the bell rang and it was the postman, we all sank a little. What happened to the parents? They seemed pleased about our move when we talked with them. All that planning, the food, the rushing to get things in perfect condition. We threw a party and nobody came. Utterly disappointing.

I remain hopeful that our new location will mean that parents will feel more welcome and will drop by more frequently. But my belief that this location is perfect for us is considerably shaken. Tomorrow, we will ask a lot of questions. Maybe we'll come up with something positive to build on.

Meetings

The Importance of Place and Setting

In the planning phase of "With and For Parents," we talked with a handful of parents who, at the time, were considered to be active members of the school's PTO. We wanted to learn their perceptions about the school as a welcoming and supportive place. These were parents recommended to us by the school's Chapter I parent liaison and the principal, the "exemplary" parents, the ones who volunteered at the school, attended meetings, represented the school at city-wide functions and were highly visible on the school's campus. We would have liked a broader sampling, one that included some parents who rarely came to the school and were *not* members of the school's parent organization, but we were new to the community and depended on the school to assist us in finding parents who would be willing to talk.

One afternoon staff members and parents piled into the car and went to a Chinese restaurant to talk about parental involvement. We were pleas-antly surprised by the frankness of the discussion, and we learned far more from this "elite" group about what keeps parents out of the schools than we had expected. One of the key reasons these parents became so involved was a belief that if they did not keep a high profile at the school and stay in close touch with what was happening, things would go downhill for their children. Interestingly, these mothers all had daughters at the school and all voiced deep concern about their safety and preventing teen pregnancy. We concluded that their protectiveness was the driving force that pushed them beyond any misgivings they may have had about intensified involvement with school at the middle school level, the time when many parents pull back. These women were also strict in their approaches to discipline and became active in order to keep an ever-watchful eye on their girls while allowing them to participate in some recreational and enrichment activity at the school. One parent told us, "I am up here every day and will continue to be until she [her daughter] finishes here." Each parent spoke very highly of the Chapter

I parent liaison and looked forward to occasions to get together with her and the close knit group of active parents.

These parents attended an incredible number of meetings and parent-focused events under the auspices of Chapter I, both at the school and district-wide. There were trips to the state capital to "lobby" for education and to meet with representatives. We were invited to attend one of the "Lobby Days" and did participate. At that time, the project had not opened its office, and we were still in the planning phase. Traveling on the bus to Annapolis from Baltimore with parents from several public schools gave us an opportunity to discuss how they felt about the schools. Some of the parents we talked to were remarkably well-informed and had specific questions and concerns to convey to their representatives. Others did not fully understand what the day meant and how to best use the opportunity. They were unclear about the goals for this event, evidently having been recruited to ensure adequate numbers of parents.

Chapter I-sponsored parent events ranged from formal and highly structured to more casual and some purely social. Always in attendance was this select group of parents who could be counted on to participate. They became envoys for the Harlem Park Middle School. They were referred to by the school staff as "our best parents" and were made to feel as though they occupied a prestigious role in the functioning of the school. Unfortunately, while the school considered the group a real asset to its parent organization efforts, many parents who were not a part of this "elite" viewed these parents as handmaids of the administration and not in touch with most parents' concerns.

We wanted to know several things from these parents who had overcome many barriers to being involved in their children's school life and who were considered "model" parents.

We were direct in asking our questions. It appeared to us, from their reactions that they had never been asked these types of questions before. Despite their personal motivation and determination to be involved, they acknowledged that the school itself did little to encourage parental involvement. They attributed any success in bringing parents to the school to the parent liaison. "She was the one that kept me coming up here," is the way one mother put it.

We wanted to know:

• How did they achieve that level of participation?

• What were their initial feelings about the school when their child entered middle school?

• Did the school feel like a place that welcomed parents and encouraged their involvement?

• Did they feel this school was a place where their child could be safe, do well and be successful?

• Why, in their opinion, were so few parents involved and what would they do to increase parental involvement?

- Did they feel the school listened to parents?
- Did they understand school policies and practices on discipline, placement, etc.? Were they fair?
- Did parents have an appeal process that worked when they were unhappy with a decision?
- Did they feel that their children were receiving a good education? Did they have strong views about what constituted a good education?
- What would they like to see improved at the school?
- Did they feel parents had the power to create the type of school they wanted for their children?

Parents gave extremely thoughtful responses to our questions, and we stayed at the restaurant for nearly two hours talking. We left convinced that we would not have had the same quality of discussion had we chosen to meet in the school. Even for these very involved parents who were comfortable going to the school, being in a relaxed setting, away from the school with some social aspect to the meeting helped greatly in allowing them to open up and talk freely about some important and difficult issues. The problem, of course, is that all meetings with parents can not be held in Chinese restaurants, but finding comparable settings that are friendly, warm and inviting is essential. Unfortunately, for the majority of parents we talked with, the school was not that place.

The School Building

For parents entering the school building for the first time, confronting its vastness and coldness can be paralyzing. We have seen parents come in and stop in the middle of the hallway, frozen and questioning. Which way should they turn? Many turn around and go out the door they came in—if they can find it.

These first impressions linger. For the parent who does not have someone to accompany her or is not part of a group interacting with the school, making a school visit can be a lonely and negative experience. It causes anxiety and many parents, feeling that pang of uneasiness when they walk through the doors, are unlikely to return except on a matter of extreme urgency.

Once parents have found their way to the office, they may encounter a friendly face, or they may be greeted coldly or indifferently. Parents have told us that they resented having to present identification. They feel like intruders. The school places the responsibility on parents for finding out what is required in order to have a conference with a teacher, visit a child's classroom, talk with a counselor or other administrator. Information is not provided to parents in such a way as to invite or encourage them to come into the building. Parents reacted to this lack of invitation simply by not going to the school. The overwhelming number of parents with whom we talked had negative experiences at the school and very few, if any, positive experiences. Very often when we suggested going to the school to address a specific problem her child was having, the parent would be silent. We could sense how difficult the decision was. Coming to a meeting at the school for many parents is out of the question. Regardless of how important that event is, parents will exercise their option not to attend. That is their right. If they are "summoned," that is a different story. They have no choice but to go. Unfortunately, poor families have grown quite accustomed to being summoned and will come on command, especially if there is an implied penalty for not showing up. This "summoning" does not set the best mood for an effective conference with parents: "You must report to our office, or we will be forced to take further action." It has a painfully familiar institutional ring to it. In many large, inner-city schools parents are only called when something is wrong. Far too few genuine invitations are made. And on rare occasions when families are invited, usually they have little or no input about the type of event they will be attending. These invitations do not feel sincere or relevant to a great majority of low-income parents, largely because no one at the school has made an effort to find out what parents really feel. Consequently, parents tend to ignore notices to attend the school's meetings and events. This does not mean they are not interested parents; it means they are not interested in the events the school has planned.

The "We'll Call a Meeting" Mentality

Wouldn't it be lovely if all the world's problems could be solved by calling a meeting? For those who have a professional background which includes community organizing, meetings are the foundation of any success in effecting change.

In the spring of 1988, after about a year of operation, "With and For Parents" took a hard, cold look at our pounding and relentless efforts to have parents come to meetings. We had listened carefully to what community service and school people said about their continued efforts to draw parents together at the school and in settings outside of the school and how dismal the attendance had been. We heard their lament over the lack of parent participation measured almost exclusively by meeting attendance. We nodded respectfully while people talked about all the "nifty" and creative approaches the school had used.

Parent involvement always comes down to having parents attend meetings, as though some kind of magic will happen there to turn around the academic success of students. In a school with 1,400 kids, organizers of meetings were lucky if 10 parents showed up at a PTO meeting. They agreed that the way to get parents to come to a school event was to involve their children in some way—usually as performers. That was fine, except that school people did not fully take advantage of these opportunities to talk to parents. They were not viewed as a recruitment tool for increased parental involvement. We talked more with school personnel, assessed their strategies and worked to avoid those factors which keep parents away. One of the most painful admissions for us was that while we were open to trying a variety of methods, we were deeply embedded in the "we'll call a meeting" mentality. Why did we feel we would succeed where others had failed?

- We had a different approach; we were meeting to discuss parent-voiced concerns and issues.
- We talked with parents about their feelings of being isolated and unsupported in their effort to deal with school-related matters. We shaped meetings to serve as support groups for parents.
- We encouraged parents to learn from other parents in a meeting. Our meetings would promote dialogue—we were not going to lecture parents.
- We believed in the long-term benefits of learning to function in a group and being effective in meetings. These are empowering skills parents can use in many aspects of their lives; however, parent training efforts seem to work best if they are integrated with activities which encourage participation generally.
- We were in an ongoing process of identifying parents with leadership potential who could be effective in gaining broader parent support and participation.
- A high energy, highly productive

meeting focussing on an issue parents are passionate about can convince them of the benefits of acting collectively to solve problems and make changes at the school, rather than trying to go it alone. Coming from such a meeting, parents can convince other parents of the importance of acting collectively.

Therefore, in the beginning we relied heavily on meetings and their potential for bringing parents together as a cohesive group working together toward a common goal. We were relentless in our pursuit of this ideal during the first year of the project and were thoroughly convinced that once parents attended a "With and For Parents" meeting, they would see that meetings can lead to real solutions. By having meetings in the Community Center, we felt assured of better parent turnouts than the school experienced. The Community Center would be perceived as less intimidating, neutral ground where parents could feel free to discuss the school without fear of betrayal of confidentiality or reprisal. We felt, too, that a good many parents had attended community meetings at the Center and were comfortable in that setting.

We were wrong. Our location in the community did have pluses in terms of being perceived by families as truly family-focussed and winning their trust but, as far as meeting attendance was concerned, we often shared the same dismal attendance statistics as the school. In some cases, ours were worse because we did not have the incentives of meeting with teachers or picking up report cards. Low meeting attendance for us was partly due to negative feelings families had about this particular Community Center and where we were located, and partly due to the fact that many parents simply would not attend meetings, no matter where they were held. They did not like meetings, nor did they see a relationship between going to meetings and improving things for their children. More often than not, when parents had attended meetings in the past, some good things may have been said, some plans made, but nothing happened to cause real change for the better. For many parents, meetings are viewed as a waste of time and a real inconvenience. The few parents who do attend meetings regularly soon become disenchanted. The same people come all of the time and do all of the work. There is little hope for accomplishing goals because it is too great an undertaking for so small a group of active, enthusiastic parents. Eventually, they feel taxed and overburdened with having to assume so much responsibility.

We learned a lot about how to overcome some of these negatives and make meetings more attractive to parents over the course of the project. Consistency is important in building parent interest. In the beginning, we scheduled meetings bi-monthly, usually on Thursdays, because that was when most parents we polled said they preferred them. We generally started at 7 p.m., again listening to parents about

the best time. In our notices to families we said how long the meeting would last (no more than an hour), and we stuck to that. Of course, we staff members stayed a little later for any parents who wanted to talk with us further, but it was important for parents to know when they would be returning home, and we respected the extra time the church staff put in for us in keeping the building open.

Being consistent did not mean that we were not flexible in our scheduling of meetings; we were. Many times we repeated a meeting agenda on several days and at different times of the day in order to accommodate more parents. We examined closely which meetings yielded the best attendance, what parents' reactions were to meetings, how many parents attended and, most importantly, how many parents contacted us afterwards to talk about issues raised. While we were experimenting with days, times and places, we were carefully documenting the pluses and minuses of topics and settings, and even the choice of refreshments.

There were times when parents expressed a desire to have a school official, politician, or other special speaker come to make a presentation. These gatherings sometimes took place at different locations and at different times in order to accommodate a larger turnout. Meetings of this sort took place later in the project, after the formation of the "With and For Parents" Club. They were often co-sponsored with the school, a church or other community organization and open to the community at large. Always, parents took a lead role in planning and organizing them.

Churches as an Ideal Setting

When we discovered that our location was a turnoff to many families, we quickly decided on a new one, consulting parents and other community residents about the best place.

As we listened to suggestions, one place kept surfacing. It was St. Gregory's Roman Catholic Church. We met with the Pastor and the Deacon, and they were happy to offer the use of church space to us. Our first meeting held at that location was one of our best attended. People knew the church well, most had been there and knew and liked the staff, and while most parents were not members of the congregation, they felt as though the church was truly committed to the community it served.

At first, we had some concerns about being linked with a church and a particular denomination and how that might possibly alienate parents. That was not a problem. St. Gregory's Church had a solid reputation in the community for being a safe, neutral and nurturing place. The pastor was regarded highly by the community and respected for the broad spectrum of services and support he offered families. We were worried too that the church was not close enough to the school or to our community center

office location. As it turned out, we were able to use the church van to transport parents to and from the meetings. The staff members who had cars also transported parents, and arrangements were made at meetings to assure that those parents who were walking home had a companion. Often the least likely places in a community unfold as ideal for gathering people together.

Churches in general make excellent meeting places. They are inviting, well kept and accessible. It does not seem to matter to most parents whether or not they are affiliated with a religious community. Black churches are viewed as neutral zones and, most importantly, as safe, family-centered places. Some churches have many meeting rooms ranging from small, intimate spaces to full-scale auditoriums. Of all the possibilities that exist in the community, we found the church to be the most conducive to well-attended meetings.

It is well to do some preliminary research before choosing a church as a meeting space. Some community residents may feel shut out of a particular church community which seems too middle class and detached from the area. Some denominations are more aggressive than others in pursuing persons for membership, and that may be a problem for some parents. But generally, churches are well connected with the community. We encountered only one parent who objected to coming to the Catholic church for a meeting. She felt our effort was not sanctioned by her religious affiliation. Meeting rooms in churches are generally bright, affirming places, well maintained and spacious. Most have kitchens, and some have play areas for children and well-kept courtyards. In the church where we held most of our parent meetings, the pastor and church staff were highly visible and supportive. Parents invited the church staff to parent functions and always included the church staff when planning events. Children seemed to enjoy coming to the church as well.

The church, family and school connection is a powerful one in the Black community. Historically, these are the institutions that Black families have been most involved in—they were shut out of many others. When schools were racially segregated, churches were perceived as an extension of family. It was not uncommon for clergy to teach in the public schools; that remains true today. A number of ministers in the Harlem Park community teach in the Baltimore City Public Schools and have a vested interest in education reform. Our partnership with the church was among one of our most productive in terms of parents coming to events. If it had been possible for us to have had an office in the church, we could have enjoyed much more success in drawing parents together. In an environment where there has been a steady deterioration of community activity and togetherness, inner-city churches have managed to create and maintain an atmosphere which is welcoming, supportive and safe.

Getting There and Back Safely—Reality and The Dependency Decision

On our staff, the parent coordinators, who did most of the daily interaction with parents, did not own cars. We had originally thought in the hiring process we would require parent coordinators to have cars. We had a good idea of how crippling it is not to have transportation, and we were especially concerned that the staff have the flexibility and mobility to meet with parents in the evening and to be able to assist with transportation when needed. As it turned out, not having their own cars did not cause coordinators as many problems as we had anticipated. Rather, it helped to keep us in closer touch with what families had to go through to get to and from places. Both coordinators were savvy about getting around the city using public transportation and were comfortable with walking in the community. But safety issues and transportation hassles cropped up from time to time in our project routine, causing us to pause and be more thoughtful in our planning of events and our expectations of families.

We had planned from the beginning to provide transportation for parents who needed it. We did not want to condescend or coddle, but we knew that for many parents lack of transportation could be the sole barrier that kept them from attending meetings or special events. Moving our meeting location farther from the school further complicated the transportation issue, or so we thought. Transportation is only a part of the reason why parents do not attend meetings, but it is an important part. When transportation is provided, it helps to overcome other related problems.

• It cuts down on the amount of time parents have to commit to an event—an important factor for parents who work and have several children.

• It helps to allay fears about personal safety on the streets after certain hours.

• It increases attendance in inclement weather.

• It sends a message to parents that their needs are being addressed and that they are truly wanted and needed.

• It allows parents with health problems and small children to attend.

We found that, especially when the weather was cooperating, parents who did attend meetings, for the most part, managed to get there without difficulty and actually preferred to come on their own. The real issue, however, was getting home safely after dark. Parents did not depend on us for transportation just because it was available. They made their own arrangements whenever they could and on pleasant days when meetings ended early enough for parents to walk home safely, they let us know that was what they preferred. Some parents would bring a neighbor, a friend, or older children to walk home with them. One parent introduced a friend she brought to the

meeting as her "walking buddy." We encouraged parents to brings friends, relatives and children.

Inviting the Children

Having children attend meetings with their parents was never a problem. In fact, it was a plus. Children used the time to do homework and sometimes to participate in discussion. Having children at meetings promoted a feeling of family involvement. We found that the kids really enjoyed seeing each other in the evening in an out-of-school setting. They were never disruptive. We were pleasantly surprised at how smoothly meetings ran, even when there were many small children present. Had we not made it clear to parents that children were welcome, we feel we would have had a much lower parent turnout. Several parents asked us if they could bring their children. One parent told us that she was asked not to bring her children when she came to the middle school. She said the principal told her this and from that point on she wondered if she could ever go back to the school. This was a woman with seven children, several under school age. Her middle school-aged son was running into difficulties which required her going to the school rather frequently. She was in a panic over what to do when she was "summoned" to the school to take care of the problem with her son. She had no options for child care, and no money to pay for it even if she could find a sitter. Certainly, this woman would never feel comfortable attending a meeting at the school, though she was in need of the support and encouragement a group of parents could offer. She was amazed when we told her that we would love to have the kids come and that we would pick her up at her doorstep if she needed transportation. We saw Ms. G.— through some difficult times, and while she did not attend many meetings, she did keep in close touch. The first meeting she did attend, when we began holding them at the church, was an important step for her. She brought her family, we were introduced to her other children and we learned about their school situations. There was food for the children and caring adults to talk to them about school and other things that interested them. It was a different meeting experience for most parents. And though many of the parents who were there that night did not turn out to be regulars at subsequent meetings, they left with a good feeling, knowing that we were seriously interested in families and their relationships with the school.

Perhaps some families came to meetings just to "check us out." That was fine. That night we made a lot of headway toward building relationships. Sometimes that is the most you can accomplish with a meeting, regardless of the intended agenda. It is an extraordinary accomplishment that goes a long way toward changing parents' attitudes about their role in the education of their children and reassuring parents that some educators who care about the quality of education for African-American children respect the power and potential of parental influence and involvement.

Misgivings parents have concerning the importance and effectiveness of meetings perhaps cannot be completely overcome. But with creative approaches, some of the basic obstacles to parents attending meetings can be circumvented. The whole family must be welcome, and the mentality of meetings must be expanded to see benefits beyond the accomplishment of a set agenda. We did not want parents to leave a meeting feeling that it was a waste of their time and that nothing that took place related to them in any meaningful way. We were diligent in setting a firm agenda for each meeting. We polled parents by telephone and visited their homes to find out their most pressing concerns. From what we learned, we decided on meeting topics and built an agenda that would ensure a full evening without gaps in the program. The truth is that parents were not all that concerned about how organized we appeared or how tight an agenda we presented but rather how relevant and important the topic of the meeting was to them personally. At the same time, for parents who had not zeroed in on their own specific concerns or worries, it was important that they felt that somewhere down the road, we might be the people with whom they could share their concerns and that attending meetings might become for them a viable way to keep abreast of important general education issues as well as provide a forum to speak up about those issues that affected them personally.

The Importance of Child Care

Child care is critical in terms of getting parents to attend meetings regularly or visit the school frequently. We addressed the need by simply inviting the children and planning ways to keep the younger ones occupied. Even with this accommodation, the majority of parents who kept in touch with us were not really interested in attending meetings regularly nor in volunteering at the school. They were interested in the information about the school that we could provide and our assistance with crisis intervention and referrals.

We encouraged each parent to define her own level of involvement and to participate in a way which felt most comfortable for her. We made it perfectly clear that if parents wanted to organize, meet regularly, volunteer at the school or visit the school, we were sensitive to the day care issues and would do whatever we could to assist them, including paying for a baby-sitter if that became necessary. We also allowed parents to leave younger children at our office while they took care of school business. It never became a problem. Parents seldom requested assistance with child care. But knowing someone understood and cared about their child care problems was just the kind of reassurance they needed to make attending a meeting possible. They need the same kind of reassurance from the school that they will be accepted when they bring their children. It is a reasonable expectation and one that is fairly easy to accommodate. Invitations to entire families to attend events, we found, resulted in higher attendance.

In our four years working with parents, we discovered that child care as it relates to increased parental involvement is not a problem unless we make it a problem. African-American parents generally prefer to take their children with them whenever possible. This is the best solution they have found for solving day care hassles. Parents go where their kids are allowed to go. This is why it is so important to hold meetings, gatherings, get-togethers—whatever you decide to call them—in settings that can accommodate children, entire families. A community center that has a day care facility is a good place as long as parents can be in close proximity to their kids. Parents will put up with a less comfortable place if their children can come, and if people aren't on pins and needles because children are present.

There is much talk about dysfunctional, inner-city minority families who desperately need parenting skills. This kind of thinking comes from Black as well as White professionals. There is a tendency to look at how children behave and the things they do while away from their parents and make rather broad judgments about their parents' ability to be good parents. If parent involvement activities were more family-centered, educators would have a clearer picture of just how "functional" African-American families are and how well-behaved children are when they are functioning in a family setting. Their apprehension about having children come to "parent" events would soon disappear. Parental involvement activity for African-American families must be more than just a meeting; it must be an enrichment opportunity for the entire family.

Changing Strategies

One parent told us after many promises that she would attend a meeting, "Look, to tell you the truth, I just don't like meetings, and I will probably not be attending." This gave the parent coordinator an opportunity to find out more about how some parents may feel about meetings generally. One suggestion was that we call them something else, like a gathering or get-together. We had entertained this idea previously but hearing it from a parent gave it an extra punch.

We began to talk of getting together, having lunch, setting time aside to talk, rather than meeting. We avoided such formal sounding terms as "sponsoring," "conducting" and "organizing" when referring to our gatherings. While some folks found this informal approach more appealing, others who drew their meeting experience mainly from church involvement felt more comfortable with the traditional trappings of meetings. The group who eventually formed the Parents Club

leaned toward a more formal structure of their own design. They insisted on conducting planning meetings, holding elections, and keeping detailed minutes—and they scheduled even more meetings than we on the project staff had. These parents tended to be the most assertive in establishing a mood for our parent gatherings, but even with their influence, the gatherings felt more casual to us and more responsive to the varying needs and styles of the parents.

Still, when attendance did not improve substantially, the discouraged staff reexamined its entire meetings strategy. Originally, we had been committed to drawing parents together at least twice a month to talk about issues they had identified as priorities. We later decided to target smaller groups whose children shared common problems: possible retention in grade, frequent absenteeism, suspension or other disciplinary action. Prior to each gathering we sent a personalized mailing profiling each student's achievement and highlighting the concerns to be discussed. Parents responded well to this targeted approached and even though many did not attend the gatherings, they were far more accessible and willing to make time to talk, having received the update on their children's school progress from us.

Students were usually present at these target group meetings, which were held at times suggested by parents (one was held on Saturday morning). While target group meetings did not result in a pattern of increased attendance by parents, they produced more interaction and dialogue than other settings had. The "With and For Parents" Club was formed at one of these events after parents decided to exchange phone numbers and stay in closer touch. None of these targeted gatherings was restricted; everyone was welcome; we simply targeted our outreach.

Parents Reaching Out to Parents

Initially, most parents were reluctant to exchange telephone numbers or continue communication among themselves beyond the parent meeting. The parent coordinators, in their frequent contacts with parents, introduced the idea thinking that being able to call parents with shared concerns and common experiences would provide mutual support and help parents feel less isolated. That is what we thought—parents felt differently. They were concerned about privacy, having their telephone numbers floating around, keeping problems in the home and not sharing them with others who might violate the confidence. We stopped pushing.

The "With and For Parents" Club

After nearly a year-and-a-half of experimenting with different approaches for planning well-attended parent meetings and family events, we received some positive feedback from

parents that a Saturday morning meeting at the church would be convenient. We decided to give it a try. We did not have a large number of parents at that meeting—around 8 to 10. But it was one of our more successful gatherings. Because it was Saturday, people were relaxed, dressed casually for doing chores and running errands. The mood was light and friendly, and it was at this meeting that parents decided on their own to exchange phone numbers, work together, and organize around specific objectives. They suggested a "With and For Parents" Club, much to our surprise. We had been trying to promote this idea for months with no success through our newsletter, with membership cards and other incentives.

Suddenly, when a parent said, "Let's form a club," the idea took shape, and parents began to organize themselves in a cohesive group called the "With and For Parents" Club. Parents then took responsibility for recruiting other parents, dividing lists of project participants and calling to let them know of the Club's plans to organize a fund-raising event to take kids on a summer trip. We took a hands-off approach, letting parents set their own pace and their own agenda, consulting us when they felt the need. As it turned out, parents wanted full staff participation and held most of their planning sessions at the "With and For Parents" office. These were usually lunch meetings —sometimes lunch was provided by the project, other times parents prepared and brought it.

They discussed their attempts to

reach and enlist more parent volunteers for their projects. These discussions became training sessions on effective recruiting. We all shared successes and setbacks in reaching and sustaining contact that would lead to increased and ongoing participation. There was a lively exchange of suggestions, cautions and pride in accomplishment when a new volunteer or member was recruited. The group swapped lists in order to give others a chance to reach parents who were difficult to contact. They drafted letters and made numerous phone calls, but they were not interested in making home visits.

The parent-led formation of the Club was an important step toward building an active, truly functioning parent organization at the Harlem Park Middle School. The Club elected officers and took over the responsibilities for sponsoring events, raising money and managing their account. Events were planned that were both recreational and educational—almost always directly focussed on the children. The Club asked the school administration for a parents' room in the school and was given an empty classroom to decorate and use as members wished. They furnished it with comfortable tables and chairs, a refrigerator, coffee maker and microwave oven, using a small stipend from "With and For Parents," supplemented with money they raised themselves. The parents' room hosted meetings and luncheons, and housed a parents' library of books and information about schools. The Club had about

The parent-led formation of the Club was an important step toward building an active, truly functioning parent organization at the Harlem Park Middle School.

twenty-five active members. The leadership and most active parents numbered about ten. These ten women were the backbone of the Club and kept it going.

As it often happens in groups, a few parents did most of the work. Over time, these parents became tired and annoyed by a lack of broader participation. After a while, the group became a bit exclusive. Having grown weary of failing recruitment efforts and repeatedly getting stuck with "all the work," they became less interested in outreach and large plans that included all parents, and became more focussed on themselves and their personal priorities. They limited their outreach, planned events that they could manage with a small group and became less interested in working on broader issues; however, in the third year of the project, after moving into the school, the outreach efforts were renewed with new parents coming into the school.

What will happen to the Parents Club now that the "With and For Parents" project is over? Support from the school is needed. If the school fails to support the leadership group, it will surely decline in membership and activities. It is too great a burden to carry alone.

Are Meetings Worth It?

Throughout the course of the project, we did a great deal of thinking about the effectiveness of meetings as a vehicle for achieving family goals and objectives. Although meetings were many times poorly attended throughout the course of the project, we decided they were worth the effort, for several reasons. We were the only organization in the community providing help to parents about school. As such, we needed to remain visible. For parents whose lives were often in flux, "With and for Parents" was a resource they could count on, a life line within reach whenever they needed it. Even when only two or three parents showed up, they brought six to eight children. We talked and ate together. Children were able to socialize with their parents in a setting that was safe, affirming and purposeful. If we planned for ten families and two came, we packed up cold cuts, cookies and soft drinks and sent them home with those families, addressing another true need. For many reasons that did not appear on the surface to be directly related to education, we could not abandon meetings as a mode of contact with families. The bonds we formed were an important accomplishment and helped us familiarize parents with the concept of family and community support for education. While we tried to be realistic about the payoff in terms of reaching specific project objectives, we believe our regular scheduling of meetings did make a difference, not just for parents but for students and for the community.

∞

Meetings: Some Lessons Learned

• Many parents feel meetings yield little to nothing in helping to solve immediate problems which affect their individual children.

• Parents are more likely to attend meetings when the agenda is kept small and targeted on a particular issue that directly affects their children; for example, suspension, dress codes, retention policies.

• Parents with whom we interacted seemed to have little interest in meetings or other events that did not address issues concerning their kids—they were not interested in stress management, nutrition/weight loss or other adult-focussed topics, unless, of course, their children were invited. Have these workshops, but arrange activities for children who will come with their parents.

• Parents like an environment for meetings where all are welcomed: children, friends, other family members.

• Food is an important component for attracting parents. It helps to make an event more social and informal. Parents tend not to be as interested in food for themselves. They like the opportunity for their children to have treats and a pleasant evening out in a supervised setting.

• Most parents prefer meetings or gatherings where they are able to talk and voice their concerns. They do not like reports or lectures in a highly formal setting. Those who do like business meetings tend to form the group's leadership and have had prior experience and success with meetings, usually in a church context.

• Shy, more retiring parents become more vocal and assertive over time once they realize meetings are a real forum for expression and no rigid rules govern opportunities to speak.

• When guest speakers are invited, parents like to choose and invite them, especially teachers and administrators from the school. Letters of invitation over a designated parent's signature yield a better response.

• Tell parents in advance how long a meeting will last and stick to that

Although meetings were many times poorly attended throughout the course of the project, we decided they were worth the effort.

timetable. Meeting notices should say that the meeting will last no more than forty-five minutes to an hour. Hold to that unless parents *decide to stay longer.*

• *Some parents who seldom attend meetings become concerned if they stop receiving meeting notices. They like knowing meetings are being held, even if they do not attend. Also, continue to send invitations to non-attendees; they feel left out if they are not contacted regularly about meetings and events, and may not be as accessible when needed for assistance and cooperation in other interventions.*

• *Even parents who are active and committed to parent involvement activity usually will not agree to host gatherings of other parents in their homes. Offers by the staff to help with refreshments, to keep the group small and other suggestions to make the idea more attractive, did not work for us. It may*

take literally years of trust-building to accomplish this, and then again, it may never happen.

CHAPTER VI

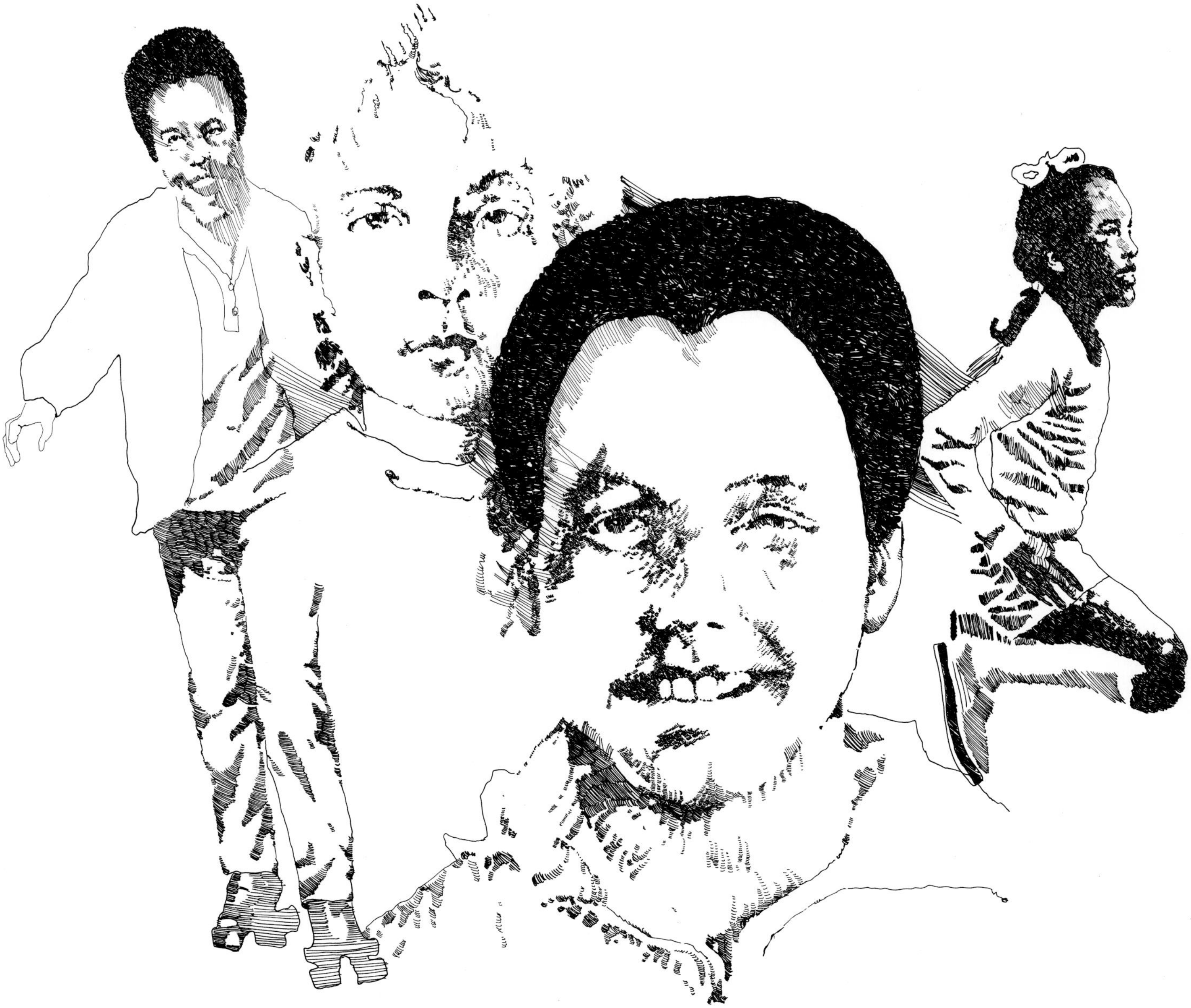

October 12, 1989

One aspect of our work I really love is writing the newsletter: selecting the perfect graphic, arranging the articles, putting together the events calendar, imagining, hoping, praying that this newsletter (unlike other parent newsletters,) will be the one parents actually read!

I am selfish about my domain. I ask for input, though sometimes, deep down, I may not really want it. The desktop publisher has become for me a miracle machine. Yes, this is the one. The "With and For Parents" Newsletter is lively, well-designed, readable and inviting. No doubt about it. We even have lovely colors of paper: deep lavender, peach, sky blue. How could this newsletter not be loved by everyone reading it? The reality is that few parents read it. If they do, they aren't letting us know about it. I suspect it is lining cat boxes or being used to swat flies. I'll bring my newsletter worries to staff meeting. Maybe someone has some creative ideas.

meeting.

Mrs.—— did not come to the meeting, but we did talk to her about her son's report card, reviewing with her what we had discussed at the meeting.

What About the Parent Who Can't Read Or Can't Read Well?

At our next staff meeting, we discussed the messages, both subtle and explicit, that we were receiving from parents. One coordinator shared with us what she had observed making a home visit:

" I noticed that Ms.—— looked at a fact sheet or flier that I gave to her. It was the way she looked at it, sort of from a distance and then she would quickly put it down. I could feel how uncomfortable she was with me standing there. I had had a feeling for a long time that she could not read. She never seemed to remember or refer to anything that we or the school had sent her. As I was leaving, I noticed a pile of mail in her foyer. I recognized some of our pieces unopened. Then I was certain. Ms.—— could not read.

It is understandable why this parent would find a meeting uncomfortable or any setting that she felt might put her under pressure to read something and "be discovered." She kept her distance with us, as we were sure she did with teachers and others. But the fact was that her child was doing poorly in school and needed some immediate interventions. We realized that this case was rather unusual in that this parent seemed to be totally incapable of handling print and, as a result, had become somewhat withdrawn. More often parents were not very comfortable with print and would tend to ignore much of what came their way. We found that many parents read material very quickly, seeming to understand what they had read but actually understanding very little. Many adults can actually read the words and extract some meaning from a text; however, they may lack the skills needed to fully comprehend and retain what they have read and to deal with unfamiliar vocabulary. They miss key information in a text and would probably not be able to use it later as a reference. It is important to design written material in a lean, clear format, carefully choosing language that will not frustrate a reader who lacks advanced vocabulary skills. We aimed for a highly readable, at-a-glance format whenever possible. At the same time, we knew that our material was for adults. It could not be condescending or appear child-like. We wanted to give information to parents that was complete, not leaving out important details but, at the same time, not being too wordy.

Parent mailings usually consisted of meeting notices, fact sheets and the project newsletter. We tried, whenever possible, to use a one-page 8-1/2 by 11 format. We frequently used graphics in our flier designs and always selected illustrations of people who resembled the people who live and work in the Harlem Park community, as well as places and settings which would feel familiar to families there.

Meeting notices were actually invitations to learn more about a school policy, to have questions answered, and to talk with other parents about their experience with the school. Having identified issues and concerns that were expressed to us by parents, we began shaping an event to focus on those issues. On the flier, concerns were often framed as questions; for example, parents told us that they were unclear about the retention policy at the Harlem Park Middle School and were uncertain from reading their child's report cards whether or not their child would pass to the seventh grade. The flier announcing the parent meeting to address this concern read: "Will Your Child Pass to the Seventh Grade?" We knew from our conversations with parents, that many would not be able to answer that question with a confident yes or no. We then listed some of the factors to consider and invited them to come to the church to discuss retention with us and other parents. We timed this flier to arrive in the homes when parents would be receiving progress reports. At the meeting, we provided parents with a fact sheet explaining the school's retention policies. We explained what major subject areas meant and how passing these courses affects a student's prospects for promotion. Additionally, we mailed fact sheets to parents who were not at the meeting.

In all of our written communication with parents, we offered several

options for more information which included calling us, dropping by the office, meeting us at the school (if that was more convenient) and allowing us to come to their homes. One of the most important mailings to parents was a flier that said, "YOU NEED NEVER FEEL ALONE ABOUT SCHOOL MATTERS. CALL US." This was one of our most important and ongoing commitments to parents.

The Parent Newsletter

Newsletters to parents were a way for us to stay visible in the home while providing parents with current information about the school, resources and events in the community. We included an events calendar in each issue and attempted two-way communication through requests for information, suggestions, news items, and interest in specific project events. We tried to keep the newsletter in a single-page format. We made it a self-mailer so that parents would not confuse it with a meeting announcement—something perhaps they had planned to ignore.

Initially, the newsletter yielded little parent response. Not until the primary responsibility for writing it was shifted to the parent coordinators, a year or more into the effort, did we get a sense that parents were actually reading it. The parent coordinators, who talked with families daily, shaped a newsletter that was more friendly, mentioning the names of parents and their children, thanking individuals for support, acknowledging birthdays, and covering a broader slice of family, community and school life. While the newsletter format remained essentially the same, the content was quite different and far more in touch with people's daily lives.

Parents were very polite about the indifference they held for the early version of our newsletter. No one said to us, "I just don't find it interesting," or, "It bores me to death." Instead, they simply did not mention it at all. But when a parent said to us, "May I have a few more copies? My daughter was so happy to see her name in the newsletter, and I want to give copies to my friends," then we knew we were on the right track and should continue. Each time we received a positive comment about the newsletter, we reinforced it by publishing similar items in subsequent issues. As time passed, the newsletter began to evolve into a parent-designed document. Sometimes this meant sacrificing material we felt was important, shortening education articles and highlighting items we may have given less attention in the past. We asked ourselves whether each newsletter was satisfying parent expectations and needs, or our own. The payoff was that parents began to read the newsletter and enjoy it.

Fact Sheets and Other Information Pieces

The fact sheet became "the power piece" we handed to parents. Each focussed on a single education issue, primarily parent-generated concerns. A fact sheet explaining a school system policy would be accompanied by a copy of that policy in its original wording, enlarged to facilitate reading. Parents had a strong interest in school system policy and school practice. Aside from the student handbook provided by the school, parents we worked with had no other source of information available to them to explain how schools operate.

School handbooks are generally student handbooks and, while copies may be available to parents (usually upon request), the purpose of these handbooks is to inform students about how their new school operates and their responsibilities. Parents are expected by the school to reinforce those rules and expectations at home and yet there is little, if any, material designed specifically for parents, taking into account not only the school's perspective, but the parent perspective as well. We wanted our information for parents to fill that gap by explaining the school rules and policies in detail, as well as the possible outcomes for infractions. We outlined steps parents could take to prevent problems at school and procedures for addressing problems that may occur, in a way that is equitable for students and parents.

We reinforced this approach to being better informed about school at meetings and in all of our interactions with parents and students. Our message was essentially that along with responsibilities there are also rights. Parents and students need to be fully informed about both. They had no idea of their rights as parents and their students' rights. We provided each parent with a "Parent Rights Card" developed by the National Committee for Citizens in Education. This card covers parents rights nationally and serves as an empowering piece. Parents put it in their wallets and carried it around with them as a constant reminder that they do indeed have rights when it comes to their child's education, and they have a resource in the National Committee for Citizens in Education to help ensure that their rights are honored. It was an important step towards parents becoming proactive about school instead of merely reactive.

It was never our intent to incite parents to anger about the school but rather to nurture a healthy concern about how well their children were being educated, to take a closer look at the school's practices, curriculum, and placement decisions and to speak out when they felt something was unjust or inappropriate.

Much of the information we designed was in response to a need by parents to know more because of a crisis which had arisen. Sometimes parents would say they had "a feeling something was not right" about a school policy or decision but not actually knowing what the written policy said, they did not feel in a position to speak up and challenge the school's position. As parents became more knowledgeable about school board policy, they generally found it fair. It was the Harlem Park Middle School's practices that they felt were often unjust and hurtful to students, especially in the area of discipline and suspension. We tried to provide parents with information about home support of education they could actually use in their lives. We knew, for example, from talking with parents at length about homework, that many parents, especially grandparents, felt inadequate helping their kids with homework in the secondary grades. They may "tell something wrong" or "confuse them, " especially in math. Parents believe, especially in the areas of math and science, that there is an old way of teaching—the way they were taught—and a new way. Believing this to be true, they felt that whatever methods they learned are outmoded, and in helping with homework, they would in fact do more harm than good. Other parents simply felt their skills were too poor to be of assistance, and some parents did not know how to monitor and assist with homework and needed guidance.

Materials we prepared about homework were sensitive to parent attitudes and apprehensions. We avoided a long list of things they should be doing daily and rigid prescriptions for the amount of time they should spend. We wanted parents to feel that they could do many helpful things to ensure that homework was completed even if they were unable to tutor or assist children with specific homework problems. We made homework suggestions that fully integrated its support into daily parenting responsibilities.

Handbooks, Pamphlets, Articles: Will Parents Read Them?

In exploring ways to format information for parents, we stayed away from long documents, choosing instead to condense and break longer information into smaller chunks. We were ready with a readable one-pager to hand or mail to parents when they needed information and as a follow-up to a personal contact. As we came to know individual parents better, we learned more about their personal responses to written literature and to what degree they valued it as a resource. We observed that some families subscribed to magazines, had books visible in the home and generally were readers of a wide variety of publications, from *Jet Magazine* to *Consumer's Guide*. This caused us to rethink our belief that books, pamphlets and articles were not the way to disseminate information to families. Like many well-intentioned people, we assumed that poor Black folks struggling to survive cannot or will not read information more than a few sentences in length. In some cases, this is absolutely true because reading, for people who don't have adequate skills, is frustrating. They understandably avoid putting themselves through the experience if they can possibly avoid it; however, this is not a universal proposition. Many poor folks do read, for pleasure as well as for information.

People generally read what they feel is relevant, what stands out and captures attention and what provides easy access to information in a non-condescending way. Pages of copy in a report-like format are not appealing to the average person regardless of race or economic circumstances. Poor quality copies on flimsy sheets of paper do not send a message that the information is important, worth keeping and reading. Unfortunately, much of the information sent from schools is formatted so poorly that it actually discourages reading. Though schools and small organizations cannot compete with the slick formats used by private industry, considerably more effort can be put into making printed materials more attractive and easy to read.

We found that parents really appreciated receiving reprints of articles from popular magazines that address parent involvement or other parenting issues. The magazine format is very friendly and accessible. Parent magazines that feature articles about school and adolescent behavior would have been even better received if they had been more focussed on people of color.

The magazines we found most in Black parents' homes were *Ebony* and *Jet*. *Ladies' Home Journal*, *McCall's* and *Family Circle* magazines that frequently feature articles of some interest to our parents were not found in their homes. They are simply too White in their presentation. We searched for supportive and motivational material from a variety of sources and found useful articles from more mainstream publications that we could make available to parents. Sometimes the entire article could be

115

We Need Parents!

To volunteer to be chaperones for kids going to Orioles Games

"With and For Parents" has been approved to participate in Operation Birdland. This means that up to 45 kids can go to selected games, free of charge, transportation provided.

In order for us to take advantage of this opportunity <u>we must have 5 adults accompany the children to each Orioles game.</u>

> **If you are interested in being a chaperone, please contact Robert Gregg at the "With and For Parents" office, the Lafayette Square Multi-Service Center, 1510 W. Lafayette Ave., 669-0400**

Parents and Kids who want to participate:
We need to hear from you soon!
The first game is June 28: *Baltimore vs. Toronto*

If Parents Don't Show, The Kids Can't Go

For further information call Robert Gregg 669-0400

 "With and for Parents" is a collaborative effort of The National Committee for Citizens in Education and the Baltimore City Public Schools

---

You Can Help Your Child at Home This Summer

Even though there may not be a lot available in terms of tutoring programs this summer, you can do a lot to help improve your child's reading and math skills.

We are in the process of organizing some helping sessions for parents in reading and math to enable you to provide structured summer learning activities at home this summer. These sessions are without charge to parents who have a "With and For Parents" membership card. There will be a one dollar charge to cover the cost of materials.

We do need to know as soon as possible how many parents are interested, so that we can begin scheduling the sessions.

If you would like to be a part of these sessions, please call Robert Gregg or Coretha Holly at the Lafayette Center (669-0400) by June 15, between the hours of 9:00 a.m. and 3:00 p.m.

> "With and for Parents"
> of Harlem Park Middle School
> Lafayette Square Multi-Service Center, Lower Level
> 1510 West Lafayette Avenue
> Baltimore, Maryland 21217

Parents: We need your news items for this newsletter.

Call "With and For Parents" Office: **669-0400**

 "With and For Parents" Is a Collaborative Effort of the National Committee for Citizens in Education and the Baltimore City Public Schools

---

You Never Again Have to Feel Alone

About

Your Child and School

Remember to <u>call</u> on us

We Are *"With and For Parents"*

Lafayette Square Multi-Service Center

(Take Ramp to Lower Level)

1510 W. Lafayette Ave.

669-0400

"With and For Parents" of Harlem Park Middle School

Parents,

We Knew You Would Be Coming So We Baked You a Cake

Join us for dessert and discussion:

✿ *Meet other Harlem Park Middle School parents.*

✿ *Talk about ways parents can get together and help our children do better in school.*

✿ *Meet our staff, talk with our parent organizers Robert and Coretha.*

WHEN: Thursday, March 10, 1988

WHERE: St. Gregory's Church 1542 N. Gilmor St.

TIME: 7 PM

We've Cooked Up Something Good for You!

See You Thursday

"With and For Parents"
of Harlem Park Middle School

Profile of a Potential Dropout
Some Characteristics

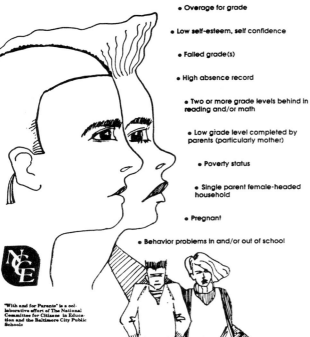

- Overage for grade
- Low self-esteem, self confidence
- Failed grade(s)
- High absence record
- Two or more grade levels behind in reading and/or math
- Low grade level completed by parents (particularly mother)
- Poverty status
- Single parent female-headed household
- Pregnant
- Behavior problems in and/or out of school

"With and for Parents" is a collaborative effort of The National Committee for Citizens in Education and the Baltimore City Public Schools

---

"With and For Parents"
of Harlem Park Middle School

Your Child's Report Card

What Numbers Spell Trouble?

Bring your child's 3rd quarter Report Card to the next meeting. Together let's find out what it really tells you.

When: April 21, 7 p.m

Where: St. Gregory's Church 1542 N. Gilmore St.

Light Refreshments served.

Return Transportation available.

Report Card		
Student:Bobbi Smith		
	1st	2nd
ART	60	65
ENGLISH	70	75
SCIENCE	65	60
MATH	70	70
REMEDIAL		
READING	70	75
PHYS ED	60	65

Parent Signature

Office: Lafayette Square Multi-Service Center
1510 W. Lafayette Ave
Baltimore, MD 21217

669-0400

Harlem Park Middle School's Team L

Invites you to attend a Conference Session with your child's teachers to discuss:

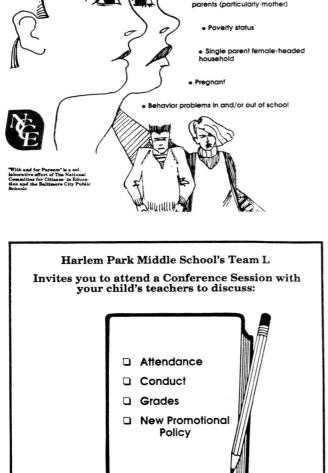

- ❑ Attendance
- ❑ Conduct
- ❑ Grades
- ❑ New Promotional Policy

**Thursday, November 10, 1988
9:15 A.M.
School Media Center (Library)**

Feel free to share YOUR Concerns!

Remember Parents, You Can Make a Difference.

**"With and For Parents"
of Harlem Park Middle School"**

Everything You Need to Know about DR (Disciplinary Removal)

(but perhaps were afraid to ask)

Parents: Come find out what you need to know

When: Wednesday, January 27

What Time: 10 a.m. or 6 p.m.

Where: "With and For Parents" office

Lafayette Square Multi-Purpose Center, Lower Level

1510 West Lafayette Avenue

669-0400

 "With and for Parents" is a collaborative effort of The National Committee for Citizens in Education and the Baltimore City Public Schools copied and handed to parents, or parts of it could be used in a packet. Rarely, did we find in the mainstream media Black children or parents featured. Even when the topics were of potential interest to all parents, regardless of race, the graphics suggested that this information was not for them. We know that issues concerning health, education, nurturing and discipline are of concern to all parents and experiences overlap for many cultures and races. And we also know that many parents would read these articles if they did not appear to be exclusively for White families.

Unfortunately, the messages many mainstream publications send are exclusive. Books for new mothers have pictures of healthy, happy White babies on the cover, rarely Black babies. Black families unfortunately are accustomed to seeing Black children pictured mostly with articles on crime, dropping out and poor performance in school, drug use or other problems. The literature that is positive, upbeat and pro-family is generally directed at White, affluent families. Therefore, it is understandable that many minority families are not as in touch with the latest findings about children's diet, health, and behavior patterns as White families are. Black families are left out of the target audience for magazine articles about improving the quality of family life. Some publishers are thoughtful about graphic design and how their publications will be received by people of color. Unfortunately, little is published in the area of parent involvement that is culturally responsive to inner-city African-American families.

It was important to us to provide parents with publications that convey the message that parents have rights along with the responsibilities everyone is so quick to assign to them. Therefore, much of the material we provided to parents, we developed ourselves. Straightforward language that clearly conveys the message of advocacy in a polished and accessible form is essential if the goal is to provide materials which are truly motivational and useful to parents. We used material developed by the National Committee for Citizens in Education, including pamphlets and full-length books.

Even if a parent does not read a book cover to cover, she feels strengthened that the information is at her disposal. Someone feels that she is important enough to have it. It represents hope and, most importantly, it becomes a part of her home. If families are to raise education to a priority level, a variety of education-related materials must be available in the homes for both students and adults. Access to information strengthens a family's faith in the ability to become an advocate for their school-aged children. Books, pamphlets and articles from national publications help to strengthen individual family connections with a national agenda to improve the quality of education for all children.

We tried to explore and utilize all opportunities for keeping parents in touch with education issues locally and nationally. Parents vary in their level of interest about education issues beyond their immediate daily concerns. We felt that the resources should be available to all parents, regardless of their level of involvement with the schools. Parents should be informed of their rights, of legislation that governs equity, and of how the school administration functions and its responsibilities for being accessible to the public and responsive to public concerns.

Will parents read all of the information provided for them? Some will and many will not; however, it would be a mistake not to provide parents with as much information as possible, under the assumption that the great majority won't read it anyway. If we are serious about the commitment to involve parents in a way that will affect achievement positively, we must make every effort to inform parents, not merely lecture to them about their responsibilities. How can we expect parents to become partners with educators when educators have so much of the important information and parents have so little?

Personal Reference Materials

By our second year of operation, we had been in many homes and talked with both parents and teachers about barriers to school achievement. One recurring concern was the failure of students to complete homework. We knew that parents were cautious about allowing their children to walk to the community library or to remain after

school to use the library. We also knew from talking with parents that students had particular difficulty completing assignments that required the use of reference materials, largely because none were available in the home. We decided to provide those references, starting with a dictionary. The volume we chose, the *Thorndike Barnhart Children's Dictionary*, could be used successfully by all children in the household.

We did far more than "deliver" it, we introduced it into the home, using the Christmas vacation to talk with all the children in the family and spark their interest in the dictionary as a reference and a source of entertainment. We designed a guide for parents to assist them in promoting use of the dictionary for homework and home learning activities.

Later, we placed in each home a comprehensive set of reference materials tailored to the needs of the high school-bound middle school student. The core collection included an information almanac, a family atlas, a more sophisticated student dictionary, a grammar and math review, and one book selected by the student and parent relating to an area of the student's interest. We found the references at this level, especially the grammar and review guides, were helpful to adults in the family who were returning to school and preparing for civil service tests. As before, we placed each collection in the homes personally, using vacation time, evenings and weekends to see as many family members as possible. This placement was considerably more complicated than the first because we wanted to have extensive conversations with parents and the high school-bound student about the new challenges lying ahead and the importance of having access to reference materials as subjects became more difficult and required more independent study and initiative. We had many long discussions around kitchen tables with books spread out to illustrate the variety of subject areas and personal enrichment opportunities. We asked that parents keep the collection in a highly visible place in the home to further highlight education as a family priority. One parent arranged the books neatly in her dining room china closet.

Rounding out the personal reference collection was a project-developed *Family Survival Kit* assembled in a binder to allow for updates. Included was information on each type of reference placed in the homes, an extensive section on Harlem Park community resources for families, and envelopes in which families could keep school documents in a safe and central place. We also provided fact sheets on ways to have effective parent/teacher conferences, parents' rights to review school records and other important parent issues regarding involvement in the schools. A grant from the William G. Baker, Jr. Memorial Foundation, a Baltimore-based community foundation, enabled us to provide the full set of reference materials to families and to develop and distribute the *Family Survival Kit*.

Reaching Parents Without Phones

Approximately one third of the families in the project were not accessible by phone. In some cases families simply did not have phones and relied solely on a neighbor or relative who would accept calls on their behalf and relay messages to them. But there were considerably larger numbers of families who had phones but who found it difficult to keep their phone service connected due to financial constraints. Many times we would call a parent whom we had been contacting by phone quite successfully only to find that the phone service has been suspended and, in some cases, disconnected. Reconnection charges were high, and some families were not able to restore their service.

As jolting as this was for us in maintaining an open and convenient line of communication with parents, we realized how disruptive suspended phone service must be for families. Being without a phone complicates every kind of contact a family needs with agencies, the school and emergency services. Using a neighbor's phone is not viewed by most families as a viable alternative since many families have not formed friendships with neighbors, and relatives do not live close by. There are not many acceptable establishments where parents can use public phones with privacy and safety. Many public phones in the community are outside, attached to taverns and stores where youths tend to gather, and are used a great deal for drug transactions. Being without a phone can virtually cripple a parent's ability to keep things going smoothly without making many trips out of the house and spending money she cannot afford. For mothers with small children, the phone may be the only link to essential resources and services.

Advantages and Disadvantages of Phone Conversations

Phone conversations were not our preferred mode of contact with families, but for many families it was the only way, at least initially, to have conversations with parents about school. We weighed the advantages against the disadvantages and decided that much of our outreach by necessity must be by phone among parents who had phones.

Advantages

• Parents do not have to leave their home to have a conversation about school.

• Parents who are reluctant or too busy to go to the school appreciate what can be learned and accomplished in a phone call.

• Many parents like phone conversations; they relax and open up a great deal more than in a meeting or other setting.

• Phones allowed the parent coordinators to reach parents in the evenings and weekends or anytime parents designated.

Disadvantages

• Some parents have negative feelings about phone calls because of experiences with solicitors, bill collectors and other bad news received by phone.

• Some parents do not feel that phone conversations are truly private and would prefer not to divulge too much information by phone.

• Many families have limited access to phones and may not receive important messages.

• With family finances so uncertain, phone service may be interrupted without our knowledge, costing several days of lost time trying to contact parents.

• With young teenagers living at home, phone lines can stay busy for hours in the evening when parents are most available.

∽

Reaching Out to Parents: Some Lessons Learned

• *Newsletters should be friendly, routine ways to keep education visible in homes, but they cannot be relied on solely to convey important information, especially that which requires parent response or action.*

• *Make communications personal and*

celebratory of individuals' achievement.

• *Often it is the case that parents who never mention any materials sent to the home, nevertheless collect them in a safe place for future reference.*

• *Families appreciate envelopes, folders or binders specially designed for them in which to keep important records. Information about the school and tips for becoming more involved should be a part of that folder. Lost documents are a frequent reason for a parent's lack of followup with the school.*

• *Parents need information about school regulations and policies in a format other than the student manual. A highly readable parents' manual should be designed for quick and easy reference. Many, many parents never receive a copy of the student manual. Creating a special manual for parents is not duplicative but essential.*

• *A glossary of education terms is useful to parents. Many parents do not understand the jargon used by schools and are therefore blocked from understanding fundamental aspects of the school's policies and decisions regarding their children.*

• *Parents do not understand how middle schools function because, in most cases, it is never explained to them. The more information they receive, the better they will feel about becoming more*

involved. For many parents, the difference between the junior high school and the middle school concept is a big mystery.

• *By necessity, important decisions about school take place by phone. Parents need to know that they can have effective phone conversations with key people at the school. For some parents, it is the only feasible way for them to be in touch on a regular basis with the school.*

• *There are many basic misunderstandings about grading, retention, grade level expectations and other policies. Parents feel that many problems could be avoided if they had the information about the school in advance, not after the fact.*

• *Parents need information that is comprehensive, balanced and non-authoritarian. Much more thought and creativity should go into the best ways to share information, instead of being selective about which information to share.*

CHAPTER VII

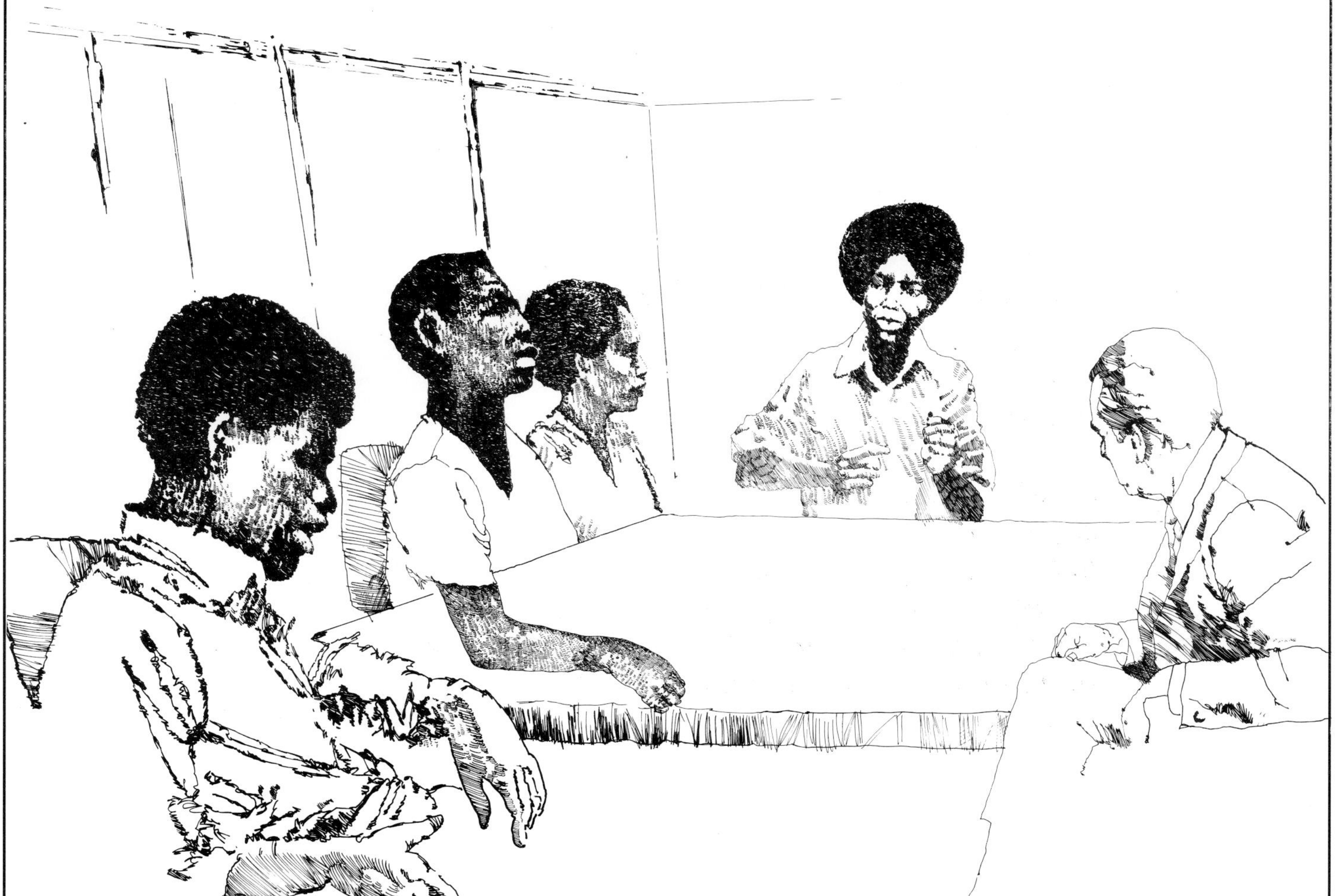

December 7, 1991

I think back on my early days of teaching, and I see so clearly now how I was operating in a vacuum and what a disservice I was doing to the students. Parents' night at the school traumatized me. Not that I didn't want to see and talk with parents, but I had this nagging feeling that I was not doing a good job of teaching their kids, especially the so-called problem kids. Part of this I blamed on the system; much of it I blamed on myself and my lack of courage. I had some creative notions about reaching kids who seemed to be slipping away, but I had very strong directives from my department head, and I was a new teacher trying to prove my ability. I really worried that young people in my classes were nearly dying from boredom and felt that none of this business meant a thing to them. I didn't know how to reach them, though I desperately wanted to.

What I did not realize at the time was the importance of reaching out to the people who were most important and influential in my students' lives—their families. Looking back, I realize that I could have confided my worries to parents as one caring adult to another. They probably could have been a great help to me. Instead of "reporting" to parents, my time would have been better spent having conversations, exchanging observations and suggestions, asking questions and doing a great deal of listening. There should have been a lot more laughter, warmth and trust.

The School

How Students Are Treated

Our first encounters with the school during the planning stage of the project caused us to focus on the school's discipline practices and the impact they had on both parents and students. On one of our early visits to the school, while we were sitting in the waiting area outside the assistant principal's office, we noticed a student, probably a sixth grader, wearing a huge dunce hat made of construction paper. He was sitting in a corner facing a wall. For a moment we were transported back in time to the days when educators made free use of tactics designed to humiliate and break the spirit of children in an attempt to keep them in line. Here we were in 1987, about to enter into a collaboration with a school that did not honor students' rights nor seem to care that parents and other visitors witnessed that blatant humiliation of young adolescents. We knew we had our work cut out for us.

Another time, again while sitting outside the assistant principal's office, we witnessed another example of harsh and humiliating discipline. In this case, a young man was leaving the principal's office escorted by a staff person and, as he was leaving, an announcement was made over the intercom system telling the entire school that one of the girls' bathrooms would be out of service because this young man was being locked in there for the remainder of the school day as punishment for entering the girls' bathroom. We could not help but wonder what the results of this discipline would be for this child. As the subject of ridicule and laughter for days, even weeks, to follow, he would have trouble living it down. How would this affect his attitude toward school, and how would he be treated by his peers? How would his parents react? Surely, it would be painful to know that your child had been made an object of laughter by the entire school.

Instruction

Of as great concern to us as the school's discipline practices were the academic approaches used with these middle school students. It was clear to us in examining the academic data of our incoming sixth graders that the system had already failed them in elementary school. A review of the reading scores for the California Achievement Test administered in the spring of 1987 showed that 85 percent of the students participating in the project scored below grade level. Seventy percent had repeated one or more grades in elementary school, twenty-five percent had been retained twice. Approximately two thirds of our students were older than the typical student at their grade level.

As we feared, low grades and declining achievement continued for our students in middle school. Despite numerous strategies with parents to help improve students' grades, "With and For Parents" was unable to significantly impact achievement. Our kids were quite open with us about their lack of motivation and interest in school. They could usually name one or two teachers whom they liked and who inspired them, but for the most part, students felt school was sheer drudgery. As one student told us—and we heard similar comments time and time again, "The only good thing about school is being with my friends"

Being in classrooms frequently and looking at the home assignments and class work required of the students, we understood their lack of enthusiasm about their studies. We found teachers often fixed in the front of the classroom, lecturing rather than teaching in an interactive style. Students were restless and unable to stay focussed. Written drills filled the chalkboards and seat work consisted of worksheets to be completed and passed in. Remediation seemed relentless, and very little teaching invited adventure and curiosity. We could look into the faces of some of the older students and know that they were counting the days to their sixteenth birthday when they put all of this behind them.

In our second year at Harlem Park, the school ended its regular school-day Chapter I services to students, This meant that students would no longer receive additional help in smaller settings in reading and math during the course of their school day. There were no after-school programs to replace the ones that had been terminated. The only Chapter I service available to students was a six-week summer school program which was voluntary. This was a devastating blow to students who were barely hanging on academically. We witnessed plummeting student grades and began immediately to do what we could to find effective and accessible supplemental learning programs for our students during the school year. There was little to draw on. Most programs were too far away, required fees too expensive for parents to pay or were not structured to provide the kind of support students needed on a daily basis to pass the subjects they were currently taking. This decision by the school system affected over fifty percent of our students and greatly impaired any progress toward increased academic achievement for this group of students. We attempted to mobilize parents to protest this action but were unsuccessful. For years parents had been so poorly informed about the Chapter I program and its goal of helping students to achieve at grade level that they did not feel any great alarm when it ended. Though Chapter I mandates parental involvement, there was little Chapter I parent activity happening in the school when we arrived and certainly none which could be considered advocacy focussed.

About one fourth of our students were placed in "special education" classrooms where the achievement expectation was extremely low. Parents were convinced that their children "had special problems" that kept them from learning and that the school was doing all it could. We found cases of students with special education placements who were in the seventh grade and unable to read and students who were scoring fairly well on standardized tests but who were making low grades and beginning to develop patterns of truancy and worsening discipline problems. We encouraged parents to insist on the re-evaluation students were supposed to receive when entering Harlem Park in the sixth grade, to ask questions about decisions for placement and be consulted in the development of an IEP. This was an awesome undertaking for some par-

ents. Understandably, they did not want to place themselves in an adversarial position with the school and possibly cause even more problems for their children. With some parents we were successful and, with our help, and in some cases, our actual presence at the hearings and evaluation meetings, they became more involved and asked important questions rather than accept what was being told to them.

The Need for Systemic Reform

Though we were in a collaboration with the school, the project's role was clearly defined as working with parents. We would have welcomed the opportunity to enter into an expanded role working more closely with teachers and staff, had we been invited or allowed to do so. But this was not within the initial terms of our collaborative agreement, and we could not force the issue without jeopardizing our access to the school and whatever level of cooperation and interest in our work we had managed to obtain. We did what we could as outsiders to help influence the school's commitment to reform. Essentially, we had no authority to transform our recommendations into school practice or policy. We were neither invited to participate in, nor informed of any special initiatives to address the critical need for restructuring to better accommodate the needs of children in this community. We were not involved in school-initiated efforts to address the issues of curriculum, tracking, testing, placement and discipline; as far as we know (and we were careful observers), there were none that invited any parent or community participation. We discussed reform issues with the school staff, mostly on an individual basis, and were convinced that we would not be successful in spearheading any reform efforts that would stand the slightest chance of success in terms of collective staff support and interest.

We knew from the beginning that there were areas in need of great improvement. We chose to collaborate with Harlem Park Middle School because of the programs already in place there to provide services to children needing additional nurture and support. We entered Harlem Park Middle School optimistic that there was much to build on and much to complement our work. What we actually found at the school conflicted with what we knew about programs and innovative strategies for better serving the needs of African-American children in disadvantaged urban communities.

Still, we recognized individual teachers and staff who deeply cared about children's needs and made genuine efforts to create a healthy, nurturing environment for learning and development. We were happy to be the conveyors to parents of good news teachers shared about students. But this happened far too seldom. We found that parents who received good news about their child tried much harder to stay connected and involved in their child's

school life. It was like an instant renewal; suddenly, feelings of frustration and futility were replaced with hope. A parent needs to hear that her child has a pleasant smile, or that she is admired by her peers, or that he has a polite and gentle manner. We have witnessed such basic compliments bring tears to a parent's eyes. For most parents, these reinforcements were rarely or never heard.

As we got to know parents, we learned that they wanted better communication with teachers but were unsure how to avoid confrontation and bad feelings. More often than not, parents were called into a conference to be told their child was doing poorly in school. Their reaction was often anger, a defense mechanism that teachers mistakenly thought was directed at them. What parents were really feeling was guilt, hurt and inadequacy. Teachers dismissed parents as being uncooperative, and parents thought teachers were actively avoiding conferences. The situation was complicated by the fact that most parents had no idea of teachers' schedules and the best way to plan a conference.

All of us in the project openly acknowledge the difficulty of running a school for children who have the problems our children have; however, all too often, school practices worsen problems, if not immediately, then certainly down the road. We found a lack of vision and faith in the potential of kids and their families to be among the greatest barriers to educational achievement and parent involvement.

Barriers to Parent Involvement

Harlem Park Middle School conducted little creative outreach to draw parents into the school and make them feel they were part of the school community. For the most part, when the school did reach out to parents, conventional strategies—parent/teacher meetings, open house events, report card pick-up days—were used. Letters sent home by students were the primary means of contact. Needless to say, these methods were not very effective. For most parents, these school events were viewed as unresponsive to their concerns and needs. The school's solution to poorly attended meetings was to have fewer of them. No one seemed to miss them—neither parents nor staff—and the school's ongoing assertion: "We invite them but they never come," was reinforced.

When we arrived on the scene, there was no newsletter for parents, no active PTO or PTA, no routine forms of communication from the school into the homes and no parent or community involvement initiatives or special projects, except for Chapter I. If the school's Chapter I liaison had been allowed to perform her parent involvement duties, she would have been able to make considerably more headway in recruiting parents to the school and in helping to organize activities that were of interest to them. Unfortunately, her duties included acting as a teachers' aide and substitute teaching. In our second year at the school, she was released totally from her parent involvement responsibilities and reclassified as a teacher's assistant.

Parents at Harlem Park needed more than invitations to a PTO meeting or other official event to feel welcome at the school. For one thing, they would have liked the school's facilities open for their use: the gym, the library, meeting rooms. Schools that shut down completely at the end of the school day virtually shut out parents and community. Recreational and social activities for families are absent from most urban schools where the need for such activities is great. A closed school sends a message of fear about the community, a message parents with children in that school do not want to hear.

We understand quite well the difficulty of convincing parents that there were benefits in coming to meetings, that schools were opening their doors to parents and community and that, with persistence and hard work, parents and educators could work together to help children be more successful. Harlem Park Middle School is like so many others; staff may say the school is open to parent involvement, that it wants to work more closely with parents, that it welcomes a greater parental presence and that it values parents as partners, but it continues to send messages to parents to stay away unless called. And that is exactly what many parents did. They stayed away from the school, disassociating themselves from school-related activities and visiting only when a crisis arose. For years this has been the way schools felt it

129

should be. Parents have been limited to a role, prescribed by the school, in which they are expected to do as they are told: obey and respect school personnel—the same thing their children are being taught.

Our parent involvement program was in a particularly precarious position because it was based in the community, working outside the school with a constituency largely ignored and mistrusted by the school. Our difficult work was further complicated by the school's failure to endorse strongly our focus on families in a dropout prevention initiative. In many ways, we were in the same position as families themselves—on the outside trying to get in.

It would not be fair to say that the school consciously thwarted parent or community attempts to access the school or actively engaged in strategies to distance parents and the community. Much of what kept parents away was not, we are convinced, deliberate. For example, we feel it was not a conscious decision to make the parent room inaccessible by locating it at the end of a long winding hall, as far away as possible from the main office and entrance. However, there was no thought given by the school staff to the kind of message that sent to parents and to project staff. As far as the school was concerned, it offered an available space; they thought little beyond that.

A parent lounge, room or center near the front of the building would have made more sense. Parents who are waiting can be offered a comfortable place to sit, have coffee and read a magazine. Our parent outreach person (formerly a parent in the project) decided to pursue this with the principal of the school. As she pointed out, "A parents' room located in the middle of nowhere just doesn't get used by parents."

Many parents will, by necessity, visit the school to deal with unpleasant matters. Schools can mitigate the tension of these conferences by welcoming parents and having secretaries acknowledge them in a friendly way, offering a comfortable place to wait and seeing them in a timely manner. Instead, teachers and administrators sometimes treat parents as the offenders. They seem to blame parents for the scrapes their children get into. The conference becomes a reprimand for parents as well as students. Understandably, parents choose not to set foot in the school if they don't have to.

It became obvious after spending time in Harlem Park, that some teachers and staff consider kids an asset and demonstrate that in the way they interact with children. Those warm, nurturing attitudes need to be extended to the parents. Some staff members at Harlem Park welcomed and encouraged parents to become involved, but unfortunately blamed parents for not being involved. Parents felt guilty enough about their children's lack of success in school without being blamed for it. When PTO attendance was low, parents were blamed for not being interested in their children. The truth was they were not interested in the PTO.

Staff people who treat parents rudely, who persist in being authoritarian and verbally abusive should be held accountable. We have witnessed at Harlem Park the damage from this type of behavior. The reputation of rude and unresponsive staff spreads quickly in the community. Parents, wishing to avoid a negative encounter, simply stay away. Parents who are not informed about how the school works and what their rights are, tend to avoid school contacts as well. Harlem Park, like other urban schools, needs to look closely at the reasons why parents are reluctant to be more involved and take responsibility for change.

The School: Some Lessons Learned

• *Parents feel that they are not really welcomed at the school despite the increased discussion about the importance of parental involvement.*

• *Many of the recommendations teachers make to parents for home support activities are not carried out because they are not accompanied by explanation and follow-up from the school.*

• *Parents want to hear strong messages of welcome from the school leadership. It is important that the principal says that he wants parents in the school and*

that all questions or problems they may have be addressed in a timely way. When the principal reaches out to parents, more parents respond.

• *A person at school should be assigned to work only with parents. That person should have flexibility to leave the building to visit parents and should not be required to "fill in" or do other duties for teachers that are not specifically parent-related. He or she should be trained to inform parents of their rights as well as their responsibilities.*

• *While parents understand the need for security at the school, they want to be treated as though they have a right to be there.*

• *Parents need to hear something positive about their children. They tend to avoid conferences with teachers because of fear they will bring more bad news. Positive, upbeat messages about students and the school generally help to ease the tension parents feel when having to go to the school.*

• *The community cares about the school. People would like to be invited in, to know more about education issues and to be supportive of school-related activities. Most people feel that schools are at the core of community life and progress. Community organizations welcome presentations from the school and newsletters that focus on education issues.*

131

• *Parents would like their children to have access to school facilities in the evenings. The school may be the only place where kids can participate in structured recreational and enrichment activities. Adults would like to use the school facilities as well.*

• *A parent room at the school is important if parents are to feel that indeed they have a place in the school. The parent room should be designed by parents; it should have what parents want, not what the staff thinks is appropriate. If parents want a television or sewing machine, that is what they should have.*

• *Parents would like to be consulted more. They appreciate being asked questions about their children, instead of constantly being told about their children. After all, who knows the student better? Many parents feel the school is harshly critical of their ability to be good parents. Parents need to be acknowledged by the school as the most influential and important people in their children's lives.*

CHAPTER VIII

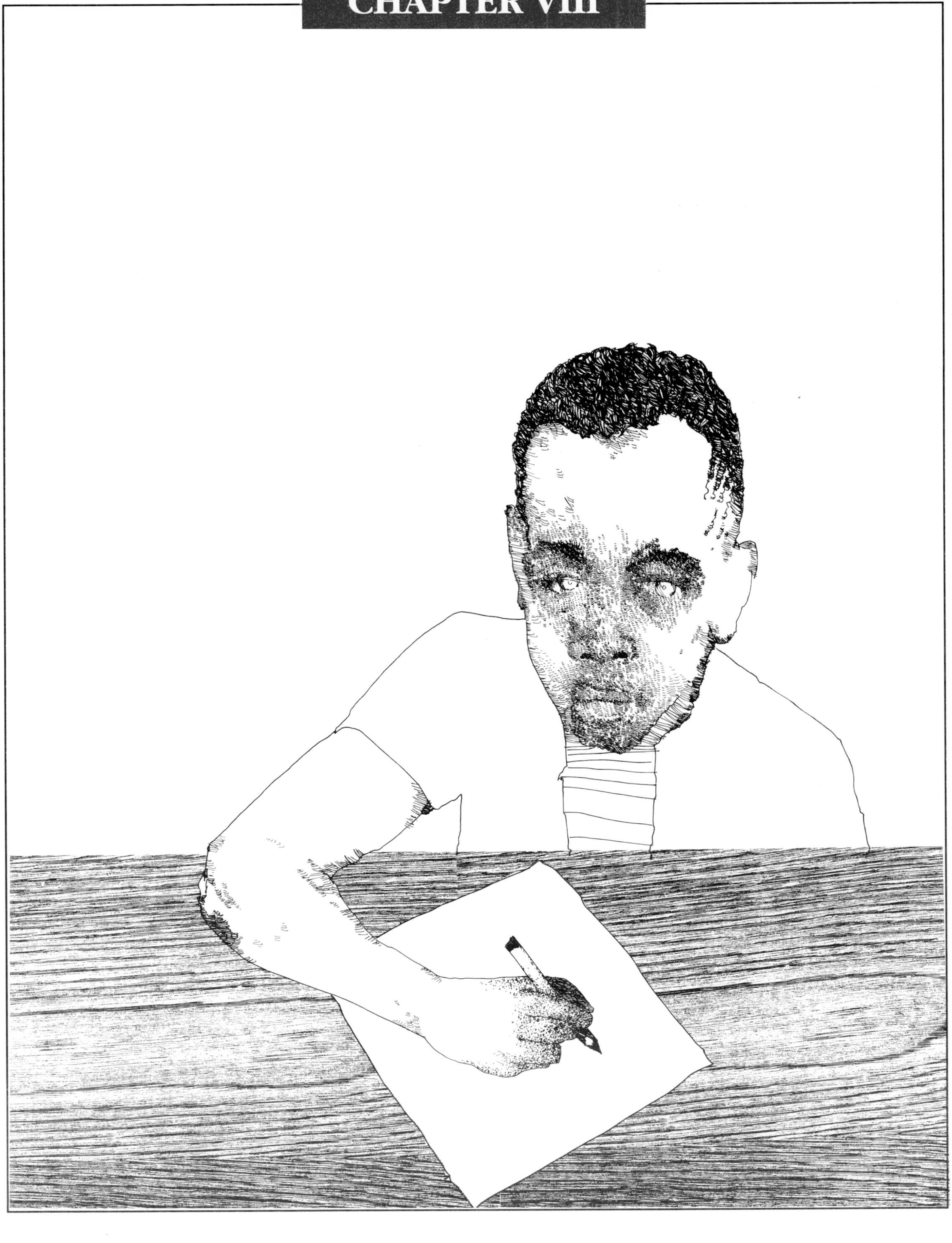

May 7, 1991

The first Monday of each month is a long day. The Lafayette Association meeting begins at seven in the evening and often lasts until well after nine. All of the politicians make an appearance. Representatives from the Mayor's office and other government agencies come to speak; several committees give their reports, and community members articulate their concerns, worries and complaints. We try never to miss this meeting—our presence is now expected. This is the place to find out who is planning to build in the area, if new low or moderate income housing is available, what new programs are proposed for the community and what progress is being made on community initiatives.

Last night's meeting was one to remember. A nervous city official faced an angry group from the community who felt they had been given the run around—"enough is enough," they told him. Just as he was beginning his response in an attempt to appease them, someone rushed in to announce that a small blue car parked outside had just been stolen. The speaker continued talking to the crowd who became very distracted by the alarming announcement. Soon, there was a mass exodus of car owners from the auditorium to check on their vehicles. Still, the speaker plowed on. Only when someone identified his car as the one stolen did he make a hasty but apologetic departure. The meeting, however, was not adjourned. It went on for at least another hour.

Finding Community Partners

Outreach to Leaders and Agencies

From the beginning, we had a commitment to the Harlem Park school and community to build a program that would encourage and support family and community involvement in the Harlem Park Middle School. In return, we hoped the program would become self-sustaining, responding to the needs of parents and citizens who wanted to play a more active role in the educational life of the community.

The formation of the "With and For Parents" advisory committee during the first year of the project provided important linkage for the program to the community and enlisted 12 influential citizens as advocates for parents. Members included the U.S. Congressman for the district, the chair of the Baltimore City Council education committee, the director of education from the Baltimore Urban League, a long-time Harlem Park resident and community

activist, the president of the largest and most active neighborhood improvement association, two clergymen, a community business owner, the principal and the director of counseling of Harlem Park Middle School and two parent representatives.

With the assistance of the advisory committee, the project gained easier access to policymakers and school system leadership. The advisory group endorsement helped to open doors for more expansive community support and recognition which, in turn, broadened the range of referrals we felt comfortable in making for parents.

Though turf struggles were evident among community groups, there was a clear need for bridging between programs doing good work for youth. Our intensive efforts to find supplemental service for families, but especially for kids, brought us in touch with other programs—some church-based, others school-based. Many wanted us to advertise their programs and promote their services to families. Others saw

value to them in having us learn more about their programs and specific eligibility requirements in order to make better-informed referrals.

In the later stages of the project, we enjoyed enrollment privileges in other local programs for "With and For Parents" families because of the relationships we had built with community service providers. We earned a reputation in the community as people who were willing to give as well as take, which resulted in an informal barter system working to the advantage of families. For example, we would agree to use our office as a pick-up point for kids enrolled in camp or other special recreational programs. In return, we would be assured that our kids could enroll and have transportation provided. This, of course, meant an extra allocation of staff time to assist in filling out applications, returning them by the deadline and then, when kids were enrolled, making sure they had what they needed for full participation (swimwear, lunch, spending change, transportation, adult chaperons, parental consent) and then supervising them daily at the bus stop.

On many occasions we bargained for preferential consideration. Usually it was granted because of our close connections with families and our willingness to reduce the chance of program no-shows. When the requirements for eligibility in a summer program included referral from another "agency," we used "With and For Parents." Networking with other agencies was labor intensive but essential to provide what

parents told us they needed.

Transition to the Community

As we drew closer to the time when our funding would end, we began to discuss ways to achieve the program's continuance as a community-owned project with parent, school staff and community leadership. The idea was well received, and we felt hopeful that we would find partners in the community willing to assume leadership. As we entered our third and final year of funding, we established some important objectives in order to garner community support:

• Becoming even more visible in the community, including increased participation in community-sponsored activities and events
• Reaching out more to community leadership for participation in project-sponsored educational activities
• Increasing contacts and dialogue with area churches, especially those active in community work
• Disseminating "With and For Parents" materials and literature to a wider community audience
• Consulting community residents and professionals serving the Harlem Park community about strategies that would best ensure continued community support and interest beyond the National Committee for Citizens in Education's presence
• Opening discussions with the Balti-

more City Public Schools about ways the central office can assist in promoting the "With and For Parents" concept within the system

• Relocating the "With and For Parents" office to a highly visible, community-owned and operated space.

In October 1990, the project moved into the Harlem Park Middle School. This decision was reached after an extensive search in the community for a suitable location and several discussions with the school principal and other community leadership about our plans to relocate. We had offers from community service agencies to share space but chose to relocate to the school at the principal's invitation. We felt this would assure greater access to incoming parents and encourage interested community people to come into the school building. It was not an easy decision to make, knowing how reluctant many parents and community people were about coming to the school. But after reviewing the other options available to us and keeping in mind early project objectives, which included encouraging parents and community to become increasingly more visible at the school and more participatory in school-sponsored activities, we decided that moving to the school would be the next logical step for the project, especially if we wanted to keep an active parent organization alive at the school beyond September 1990.

The senior parent coordinator for the project took over the project's leadership in October 1990 and began working to secure commitments from community leaders, interested parents and citizens, and school personnel to ensure that "With and For Parents" would continue to function as a parent/community organization to address the need for greater family and community presence in school. The Harlem Park Middle School relies heavily on the volunteer efforts of parents and citizens who work closely with "With and For Parents" to plan and implement its parent-focussed activities. A major accomplishment of the Parents Club was recruiting new members to carry on after original members' children graduated from Harlem Park Middle School in the spring of 1990. The group re-elected officers for the 1990-91 academic year and organized the parent center (an unused classroom in the school) to suit the needs of parents whose children currently attend Harlem Park.

Several parent-focussed activities were initiated, supported and implemented by the volunteers of the "With and For Parents" Club in a collaborative effort with school staff:

• A "Meet Your Child's Sixth Grade Teachers" gathering was held in the parent center for new Harlem Park families at the beginning of the school year. Responsibility for a majority of the outreach, planning and refreshments was assumed by the parent group membership.

• A general parent meeting was planned with the principal. Again outreach and planning was done by the

Parents Club.

• A "Feast and Forum Meeting" was sponsored by the Parents Club. These two self-esteem workshops, one held during the day, one in the evening, were well attended. Each included a buffet for participants.

• A meeting and discussion was held for parents of children with special education placements.

All of these activities required both considerable staff support in planning and a vigorous outreach. The families being courted were new to the school and to the "With and For Parents" concept. They did not have the benefit of the years of special attention and support the original "With and For Parents" families had received; however, many were anxious to participate in a Harlem Park school event to get a better idea of what the school was like.

In the transitional phase, throughout the 1990-91 school year, two part-time staff people kept the program going. One of the project's parent coordinators and a former parent in the project assumed the responsibilities for clerical work and for parent and community outreach. These two deserve enormous credit for undertaking a major responsibility with few resources. They worked diligently to maintain a "With and For Parents" presence in the school while at the same time garnering support in the community.

Progress in the Transfer of Project Ownership

What happens as a result of this final phase, during which we reached out to incoming parents and to a broader segment of the community, is an important measurement of success for the "With and For Parents" alternative to the traditional PTA or PTO. What we asked, without the offer of monetary support, was for community organizations and agencies already operating on low or no budgets to take on some of the major responsibilities associated with the daily operation of "With and For Parents."

A true test of our status in the community and integration into the community service network was our ability to draw a large group of influential community people around a table to discuss the future of "With and For Parents." This we did in the form of a continental breakfast in the fall of 1990. Discussion around the table generated the following strategies for the community's shared ownership of the program:

• Agreements to include "With and For Parents" information, newsletters, and announcements of events in other community organizations' and agencies' routine mailings

• Commitments by community organizations to sponsor or co-sponsor with the school education forums, events and activities drawing community-wide response and participation, and promoting collaborations with the existing "With and For Parents" group

• Active recruitment of community activists and professionals to volunteer to organize and oversee "With and For Parents" functions

• Release time for staff in community agencies to participate in and help to plan project activities

• Fund raising efforts to cover the cost of sponsoring "With and For Parents" events and to provide informational and promotional literature and materials needed to keep "With and For Parents" visible and viable in the community

• Shared monitoring by community groups, parents and citizens of the school's continued support of "With and For Parents."

Realizing that already-strained staff and budgets of community organizations would restrict our ability to gain concrete commitments of time and resources, "With and For Parents" worked with the community to negotiate ways to share responsibility for the program that would not overburden any one organization, agency or group of volunteers.

For the academic year 1990-91, "With and For Parents" functioned as the parent organization for the Harlem Park Middle School. During this time, continuing coalition-building efforts increased community support and participation in parent involvement activities at the Harlem Park Middle School. A "With and For Parents" community newsletter entitled *EDUCATION MATTERS* was published bimonthly and was well-received by parents, shopkeepers, clergy, community workers and other

citizens interested in the educational life of the community. As a result, inquiries and interest in "With and For Parents" increased dramatically. The principal of Harlem Park expressed interest in keeping the "With and For Parents" Club operational, as well as an openness to seek shared community and school staff responsibility in order to maintain an active membership.

The Final Phase

On March 15, 1991, the National Committee for Citizens in Education received a small grant from The Prudential Foundation for support of the transitional phase enabling project staff to remain at the school until June 30. The National Committee for Citizens in Education's commitment to the project ended at that time.

We feel that we have experienced some success in this final phase in raising project visibility at the school and in integrating the project's initiatives into the mainstream of community activity; however, the success of "With and For Parents" as an independent parent organization working closely with the Harlem Park Middle School and community remains to be seen.

We have considerable optimism about the perpetuation of "With and For Parents" and the continuance of parent and community involvement activity at the Harlem Park Middle School. The "With and For Parents" Club continues to be the parent organization at the school. Project representatives have gone to each feeder elementary school along with school staff to introduce the "With and For Parents" idea to parents of incoming sixth graders. The parent room set up at Harlem Park Middle School by the Parents Club continues to be a lounge and a place where parents can hold gatherings and workshops. Most importantly, a firm foundation has been laid by parents for the type of organization they want. They, not the school, select its leadership and set its agenda. The organization enjoys high visibility and support from the community. Members know they can call on people of influence, including former advisory board members, for assistance, if they need it.

A community service network that has worked successfully with the program for four years now knows the value of working closely with parents in any programs that serve children and in integrating education issues in the primary work they do with families.

Still, there are no guarantees that the program will continue. The National Committee for Citizens in Education has done what it could during the 42-month project to lay the groundwork for a continuing parent effort. The mechanisms are in place; now it is up to the school and the community to provide the setting and the support to keep the parent/community involvement wheels turning.

Summary and Accomplishments

Concern and Hope

"With and For Parents" was a dropout prevention program focusing on parent involvement. Our dilemma as staff members was to fully integrate critical dropout factors into every aspect of our work with parents without inadvertently sending the message that dropping out seemed inevitable, given the circumstances of the majority of our students. Because there were parents in the project who had themselves dropped out of school and who had unsuccessful school experiences, we took special care to present information about the crippling effects of dropping out on a student's future. Yet we could not, in good conscience, withhold information, no matter how discouraging. We wanted parents to have access to the same knowledge about dropouts that educators, politicians and policymakers use to make predictions about the futures of African-American children living in poverty. We worked to shatter the myth that poverty and ignorance go together. We approached parents with a balance of concern and hope.

Project Impact on Mobility

We expected to lose some children and families over the course of the project due to family moves and student transfers. We decided not to seek replacements for those who left Harlem Park Middle School, either in the experimental group or the control group, but to measure dropout-related outcomes only for those in the original groups who remained in the school.

One of the most striking findings from an examination of data at the end of three years was the evidence of less mobility among the "With and For Parents" students. As most students prepared to enter high school in September 1990 (13 in the experimental group were retained in either 7th or 8th grade), 109 of the original experimental group of 156 were still being tracked by the Baltimore City schools, whereas only 80 of 151 remained from the control group. By the end of the fourth year, three more students in the control and three in the experimental group had withdrawn from the Baltimore City Schools. One student, we know, received a scholarship to a private school out of state. The others either moved or quietly stopped attending school. None of these students had reached their 16th birthday and so were not old enough to officially quit school. They were listed as "withdrawn" and, in some cases,

Student outcomes for 1990-91 school year
(Source: Baltimore City Public Schools)

	Beginning enrollment Sept 1990	Dropout	Withdraw	Ending enrollment June 1991
Experimental group	109	7	3	99
Control group	80	6	3	71

"whereabouts unknown," not as dropouts.

The student count data produced by the school system over the summer of 1991 is not 100 percent accurate. Ten "With and For Parents" students were not included in the printout, although we knew their whereabouts from checking with family members. Five of these students had matriculated at Harlem Park Middle School in June 1990 but were not listed. They were special cases who left Harlem Park in the prior year to enroll in residential drug treatment programs, detention

based on the data received from the school system. But it is noteworthy that our experimental group had a much higher rate of mobility during their elementary school years: sixty percent had attended more than one elementary school and thirty percent had attended three or more schools during their K-5 years. We believe the significant difference in "survival rates" for the two groups demonstrates that involvement in the "With and For Parents" project helped create a greater sense of student/parent belonging at Harlem Park which may

Changes in size of experimental and control groups between September 1987 and September 1990
(Source: Baltimore City Public Schools)

	Beginning sample Sept 1987	Ending sample Sept 1990	% change
Experimental group	156	109	30

centers and group home environments but later returned to Harlem Park Middle School. Somehow, they were lost in the system. We suspect that the control group had similar cases, but we do not have the same avenues for tracking these students as we do for the experimental group.

It is difficult to assign exact causes to the difference in rates of attrition

have modified the typical mobility patterns for families in that community. The feeling of empowerment parents gained over their children's education may have made a difference in terms of their desire to keep their child in the school.

Often we tried to deter a family from moving or transferring their child from Harlem Park as a solution to school-related problems. After talking things through with us, they were sometimes convinced that a transfer could ultimately increase the risk that their student would not remain in school until graduation. We were able to find assistance with transportation costs for several families who did relocate, allowing their children to stay at Harlem Park Middle School without additional financial hardship.

Dropouts and Pushouts

In the fourth year after "With and For Parents" came to Harlem Park (when the original 6th graders should have been attending their first year of high school) seven in the experimental group and six in the control group dropped out of school. All were 16 and overage in their grade. In Baltimore, overage students with poor attendance may be dropped from the rolls after sixteen consecutive absences. These students did not necessarily make a conscious choice to drop out of school. One parent told us, for example, that the principal of her son's high school asked the sixteen-year-old to leave because he was making the other students in his class uncomfortable. Another family told us that students who supposedly "dropped out" were looking for ways to be legally reinstated in the system. We do not view these overage students as "dropouts" but as "pushouts." Now it is largely incumbent on them and their families to find a place where they fit into the system. Most view this process as

degrading and frustrating. Little help is offered from the school to encourage students to remain until they receive a diploma. The system seems more relieved than concerned when these students fall off the rolls.

As discouraging as the news was on dropouts, we took some comfort in the number of overage students who remained in school. During the 1990-91 school year, 38 of 45 overage students in the experimental group (85 percent) continued in school. The rate for the control group was nearly as high, with 25 of 32 overage students (80 percent) still enrolled in June 1991. These figures represented a much lower dropout rate for students in both the experimental group and the control than for the system as a whole. While our Harlem Park students averaged a 7 percent dropout rate, city-wide the dropout rate for the ninth grade is 17 percent. We attribute the better-than-average rate of school continuance among students remaining in our pool to the positive impact of their remaining at one school throughout their middle school years. Though we did not track the students who left Harlem Park during the three years of the project, we feel it safe to speculate, given what we know about their elementary school history and time spent at Harlem Park Middle, that the dropout rate among the students who left that school may be significantly higher, due in part to their greater mobility. Adjustment to a new school (especially mid-year) can have a negative impact on grades and increase chances for future retentions. Both poor grades and retention significantly increase the risk of dropping out.

Conclusive data of the project's impact on the dropout rate will not be available until 1994, the projected year of graduation from high school for the majority of the "With and For Parents" students. Although the project has officially ended, NCCE will be able to report these results with the assistance of a federally funded Chapter 2 block grant which the city will use to track dropouts. If the lower dropout rates continue for the experimental and control groups, the project will have established an important correlate for school staying power: lower family and student mobility.

Attendance

The information we provided to parents about how the Harlem Park School operates enabled them to explore long-range strategies for dropout prevention which they would not have otherwise considered. For example, parents formerly may have chosen to deal with a conflict at school by advising their child to stay home and "cool off," hoping the climate would be better when the child returned and the incident could be forgotten. We helped parents see that this approach meant that valuable learning time for the student would be lost and that an opportunity would be missed for parents to meet with school personnel, discuss what actually occurred and decide what steps could be taken to avoid similar problems in the future. With our urging and support, parents became far more interactive with the school and more determined that their child should lose as little learning time as possible.

Though our efforts did not decrease the rate of absenteeism for the entire sample group, we know that some students would have lost far more time from school had alternatives not been presented to their parents. Absentee rates for both the experimental and control group overall showed a steady increase as children grew older. The percentage of students absent 0-20 days per year decreased in both groups and the percentage of students with more than 50 days of absence a year increased steadily in the second, third and fourth years. The only positive conclusion we were able to draw from this data is that the students did remain enrolled in school despite poor attendance. Without the intensive work with families provided by "With and For Parents," marginal students with 50 or more absences might have left school in the eighth or ninth grade. In fact, this could help explain the lower number of students remaining in the control group at the end of four years. Perhaps many of these families had not moved out of the attendance area at all. Without special efforts to keep them in school, many of the students with poor attendance records may simply have left, even though they were not yet sixteen.

Academic Achievement

The improvement our students experienced in academic achievement over the course of the project was individual rather than collective. As a group, grades for math, social studies, language and science, which had averaged in the mid-70s in sixth grade, declined by four points by eighth grade, to barely passing. While language skills as measured on the California Achievement Tests (CATS) rose to near grade level by the end of eighth grade, progress in reading and math was not as great. The control group, on the other hand, bridged the grade level gap in math on the CATs

significant impact on student achievement. Two examples make the point:

Student A entered Harlem Park Middle School two years overage. There he was retained again due to failing grades and a poor attendance pattern carried over from elementary school. Although he was three years older than his classmates in seventh grade and struggled to keep up with his school work, we managed, with the help of his guardian (an aunt suffering from crippling degenerative arthritis), to persuade him that hard work and persistence would pay off in his graduation from Harlem Park and admission to a city-wide high school.

Absence rates for experimental and control groups:

September 1987-June 1990

(Source: Baltimore City Public Schools)

Absences per School year	6th Grade		7th Grade		8th Grade		9th Grade	
	Exper	Contrl	Exper	Contrl	Exper	Contrl	Exper	Contrl
0-10	29%	31%	25%	23%	24%	23%	15%	19%
11-20	19%	21%	13%	12%	15%	20%	17%	16%
21-50	29%	35%	26%	34%	28%	34%	24%	19%
51-100	20%	13%	21%	17%	20%	13%	17%	30%
> 100	3%	0%	15%	5%	14%	10%	25%	16%

but lagged behind in reading and language skills at the end of the eighth grade. Their grade point averages in major subjects also declined over the three-year period.

As disappointing as these results were to us, we can document a number of individual cases in which, because of our assistance, advice, interventions and advocacy, we had a

He succeeded in both of those goals, raising his grades from sixties to eighties and cutting his absences in half.

Student B entered Harlem Park Middle School one year overage and was retained in both the sixth and seventh grades due to recurring attendance, discipline and substance abuse problems, as well as trouble at home. It was difficult for him to focus on school for any length of time. We worked closely with his mother to help resolve some family tension, found treatment for the student's worsening substance abuse problems and cooperated with the school to ensure that teachers monitored his behavior, attendance and any changes in attitude. The work with this student and his mother involved many home visits, teacher/parent conferences and referrals to other agencies. Despite some reversals (including a period of worsening attendance), the student's grades finally went from failing to passing, and he was able to attend his zoned high school in September 1990 instead of the alternative school earlier projected for him.

In addition to working intensively with families of students in immediate danger of failing, we focussed a great deal of our information to all parents in the group on grades and report cards. This led to a better understanding of what their child's grades meant and resulted in discussions about grade level expectations, tests, homework and the effects of discipline on a child's grade. As a result of our coaching, parents knew what questions to ask in parent/teacher conferences. They learned to read the report cards more accurately and therefore were more concerned that their child receive a grade of at least 70 (passing), especially in remedial classes. We provided parents with a computerized printout profiling their child's grades for their entire stay at Harlem Park. This made it easier for parents to look at

grades and attendance over a period of time and to spot reversals in progress. It was then possible to discuss with parents more concretely any developing patterns that were putting their child at greater risk for dropping out of school. We consciously avoided the term "at-risk" for our students, but we felt it was important that parents understand what educators mean when they use it. We did not want parents to accept "at-risk" as being synonymous with poor and Black.

A Parent Voice

We had a dropout prevention goal for the students, but our goals for families were far more expansive. We set out to change the attitudes of low-income African-American parents about their role and influence in the educational lives of their children. An important facet of this was to reconnect those parents who had been active in the early years of their children's education with the school life of their older student and to help all parents in the experimental group expand the definition of parent involvement. Instead of waiting for the school to call them, we wanted parents to demand from the system what was best for their children, and to know and exercise their rights by law to access information about the schools and their children's confidential school records.

Our mission was not to reform the school, though we recognize the urgent need for systemic reform if schools are to educate all children equitably and prepare them to become the adults they wish to be. We chose to focus on parents and on families, to share information, to demystify the educational process and to show parents ways they can circumvent barriers to having a voice and a presence in their children's education. We worked collaboratively with the school, but families were our constituents and our first concern. It was not an aim of this project to antagonize or to fuel confrontation between parents and the school. While it was our hope that parents would organize to address shared concerns, and be assertive and vocal in their pursuit of desired outcomes, we knew that this type of collective parent initiative, if it happened at all, would occur when parents were ready. This project was not designed to be a community organizing endeavor. The primary goal was to assist parents in becoming a greater part of the education of their children, to find ways they could be comfortable and effective in their involvement, and feel strong enough to have their voices heard and their concerns listened to and taken seriously. It was our intention to help them better understand education issues, to be advocates for their children and to be better informed about where to find the help and support they needed.

CAT scores of experimental and control groups in 6th and 8th grades
(Source: Harlem Park Middle School)

| | June 1987 (end of 6th grade) Grade Level = 6.9 | | | Spring 1989 (end of 8th grade) Grade Level = 8.9 | | |
	Rdg	Math	Lang	Rdg	Math	Lang
Experimental group	4.7	5.8	5.8	6.0	6.9	8.5
Control group	4.9	5.6	5.3	6.7	8.8	7.4

Average grades for math, social studies, language and science of experimental and control groups in grades 6, 7, and 8.
(Source: Harlem Park Middle school)

| Passing = 70 | 6th grade | | | | 7th grade | | | | 8th grade | | | |
	M	SS	L	SC	M	SS	L	SC	M	SS	L	SC
Experimental group	76.7	75	76.7	75.6	71.9	71.4	73.3	71.9	71.5	72	71.4	71.5
Control group	75.5	74.5	77.8	74.9	72.4	72.2	73.5	72.2	71.8	72	71.9	72

147

Advocacy

When parents were dismissed or waved away by the school, we were there to help firm their resolve to get the answers and the solutions they wanted. We encouraged parents to assume a more proactive rather than reactive posture, to be less accepting of what they had perceived as mandates from "on high" and to view decisions about their children's education as negotiable. We also encouraged and supported proactive behavior in dealing with institutions other than the school—health clinics, the Department of Social Services, public housing, to name a few.

We were highly successful in reaching parents with the message that they had rights and not just responsibilities when negotiating solutions. Gaining access to resources and finding satisfactory solutions to problems involves more than showing up for an appointment when called, signing papers, providing requested information and then going home and quietly waiting, hoping that things will turn out for the best. Parents readily agreed that the passive approach had produced little for them, and that they felt increasingly shut out and ignored by most public institutions, including the schools.

"With and For Parents" was successful in reaching low-income African-American parents and discovering ways they could be effective. We did not go to them with a set of rules or standards defining an ideal involved parent. We did not say, "This is what parents of successful stu-

dents do, and this is what you should do, too."

Outreach to Families

Our outreach to parents was intensive, and it paid off. Logs, kept over a three-year period, show the following level of effort by "With and for Parents" staff members:

- more than four thousand phone calls to parents
- nearly two thousand visits to parents' homes
- sixty information mailings to parents
- over fifty project events for families
- face-to-face contact with 90 percent of families in their homes.

Many of the parents with whom we talked on a regular basis about school-related problems and who attended "With and For Parents" events had not had any prior relationship with the school. Sixty-nine parents (44 percent of the total project participants) attended at least one meeting.

Organizing

In our first year, we attempted to identify parents and school staff involved in the school-sponsored PTO in order to establish a collaborative relationship with our own program, but we soon learned that the PTO at Harlem Park was an organization in name only. Parents listed as members and officers no longer even had children at Harlem Park. Although there were some parent volunteers, there was no organized parent involvement effort at the school (except for that initiated by the Chapter I liaison). That situation changed as a direct result of "With and For Parents." By the time our project ended, the Parents Club was a visible presence in the school with its own activities room, treasury and calendar of events supporting student activities such as the popular Black History Month contest. Parents ran the organization, elected their officers, created their own agenda and managed their own funds. In addition to their fund-raising efforts, the Parents' Club treasury benefited from grant monies which earlier had been earmarked as a principal's fund to expand parent involvement activities school-wide. Since the principal chose not to use the money for that purpose in the first year of the project, but instead to buy equipment with it, the stipend was awarded to the Parents Club in succeeding years.

Problem Resolution

A great majority of our contacts with parents were geared to keep them informed about what was happening with their children at school. We monitored student achievement very closely and assisted parents in identifying developing problems before they worsened and interventions became far more complex and time consuming. We checked the daily attendance roster at the school and called parents when we found irregular attendance patterns. We became involved in team meetings at the school where teachers discussed the academic problems of students at length and tried to find solutions. In those meetings we represented our students and their families, listened carefully to teachers' concerns and shared this information with parents. When additional support services were needed to help students with problems such as drug abuse or severe emotional distress, we immediately worked to involve parents in the process of finding appropriate assistance for their children, rather than leaving it up to the school. We participated in approximately two hundred problem resolution sessions in which parents contacted school officials and outside agencies on behalf of their children. With the project's assistance and support, students were treated for substance abuse without interruption of their studies, found supplemental learning programs and part-time employment, and received counseling and mentoring. Without these important interventions, students would have faced long-term suspension, expulsion from school, forced transfer to an alternative or out-of-community school, retention or reform school, all of which would have increased the likelihood of their eventually dropping out.

149

Retention

As we formed working relationships with teachers and administrators at the school, we were invited to participate in retention committee hearings. This allowed us to "lobby" for our students to be promoted. We brought to the table assurances that the student would fulfill the school's requirements for conditional promotion. We lobbied especially hard for students in the project who had a history of two or more retentions and who were becoming emotionally disconnected from school. In the last year of the project, 24 students were retained. By the end of that summer, working together with parents and the school, we were able to assist with the promotion to high school of 11 of those students.

Dependency and Natural Networks

Two issues with possible negative consequences for achieving project goals for parents were raised early and continued to plague us. One was the concern that the staff was reinforcing dependency patterns by assisting low-income minority parents with everything from transportation to letter writing and problem resolution at school. The other was that the ability of parents to act for positive change might be greatly hampered by the research design; that is, by selecting and working with a sample, we ignored the "natural networks" Harlem Park parents had formed

among families and individuals outside the sample group.

While we never fully resolved either question, we are indebted to ethnographic researcher Michelle Fine, who worked with us over the course of the project, for her fresh insights into these issues. Speaking to the dependency concern, Fine reminded us that no one functions without support systems. Middle class adults pay for the repairs, child care, tutors and legal assistance they need from time to time. Some families cannot afford these services, but they should not be expected to go it alone, nor should their need for assistance be interpreted as an inability to manage their lives. "Empowerment is a reciprocal and collective process, not an individual act," concludes Fine in her evaluation of the third year of the project. "This shift in the definition and practice of empowerment is particularly important in the 1990s when so many social service and advocacy groups are hailing `self-sufficiency' as their ultimate goal. What these women [in the project] make clear is that they have been `too' self sufficient—that is, alone. The good news is that "With and For Parents" created a context which these women could rely on...."

To the question of working outside families' natural networks, we agreed that the research-driven sample made an already bad situation worse. Fine considers the extent of "communitarian damage" in Harlem Park and other similar neighborhoods to be underestimated, one result being that natural networks have been severely weakened. Add to that the criterion of a random sample, and the potential for parents and extended families to coalesce around common concerns is further reduced. As Fine says, "In the earlier design [of neighborhood projects], people used to invite others into their homes to discuss issues. Now they say they don't want anybody minding their business. There is a real distrust among adults. Walk in with older notions of community organizing that require some community trust, and they evaporate pretty quickly." We did not fail to organize parents using our research design, but it did take time for parents to become comfortable and trusting with each other to the extent that they could exchange phone numbers and work together on a regular basis. It is difficult to say whether the Parents Club would have been formed sooner or would have been stronger or parent involvement more frequent had the process been opened to all the families in the school.

We did play to family networks to the extent that we included in our outreach not only birth parents but any adult assuming responsibility for the child. We did not organize those outside the sample group but we were a resource for those who were interested in community activism for change. Several older neighborhood residents became regular attendees of our events, but we did not actively recruit from the entire neighborhood because of limited resources and a desire to

maintain the integrity of the experimental design. Therefore we cannot say that "With and For Parents" realized the full potential for parent involvement at Harlem Park.

Information for Action

Prior to our presence in the community, parents had little knowledge of the school's responsibilities to them regarding disciplinary actions, placement decisions or conference scheduling for crisis resolution. Until we suggested it, neither parents nor school personnel had explored alternatives for parents who cannot leave work to come to the school to reinstate a child after disciplinary removal (a three-day suspension from school allowed up to three times per semester). One of the accomplishments of the project was to give parents copies of school policies, the rules and regulations set by the school board governing disciplinary removal and longer suspensions, and the rights of parents to review the confidential student records maintained by the school. For many parents, the experience of learning what the school system policies stated and contrasting them with school practice changed their reaction in a crisis situation. Armed with knowledge of system policy, many parents found new resolve to deal with practices they had felt were unfair but now knew were illegal. But while parents acted assertively as individuals to fight practices that were harming their child, we were never able to convince them to orga-

151

nize as a group to challenge them.

Disciplinary removal did not go away. Largely due to our efforts, a group of other community youth-serving organizations became interested in DRs and suggested alternatives to sending children home repeatedly, especially for minor offenses. In one plan, two churches offered to staff an in-house suspension program. As a result of our pushing education issues in broader community settings that included citizens without children at Harlem Park (senior citizens, community activists and politicians), we were able to be a catalyst for reform activities without collective action among parents. This allowed us to concentrate on the daily concerns parents had—getting their middle schooler past the many hurdles he or she faced adjusting to their new, more complex school environment and pressing family survival issues that made it difficult to focus on school. While we were concerned in the beginning that we were being viewed primarily as people to call on only in a crisis, we realized that the assistance we provided helped to convince parents of the importance of initiating action toward solutions, and that persistence and follow-up are often necessary components of effective crisis resolution. During our four years in Harlem Park, we came to know firsthand the frustration of being shifted from one person to another, especially in the central office. Requests for materials largely went unanswered, and no amount of phone calls seemed to make a difference.

Helping parents learn who is accountable for what in the school system was an important step toward their understanding about how that system functions. From there they could develop a plan of action for penetrating the barrier of unresponsive school personnel.

Information was almost impossible to keep current given the frequent change in leadership both at the central office and at Harlem Park Middle School. Needless to say, if we who had a formal collaboration with the school system were encountering difficulty getting information and assistance, parents and average citizens were having an even more difficult time. In pursuit of this project's objectives, we honed our own skills with those who held important information and, in turn, shared our successful methods with families.

Parents learned as we did about whom to contact in an administration in flux. Two years into the project, the principal of Harlem Park left, and along with parents, we were among the last to know. Parents and community leaders were neither informed nor consulted about the impending change. Understandably, there was both confusion and resentment over the selection of a new administrator. Now, two years later, it is fairly certain that this principal too, will be replaced. This time though, the community has become involved in the decision, and NCCE staff will participate in discussions to help articulate the needs of Harlem Park students and families. We view inclusion in this

The Lessons of Harlem Park
William Rioux

I urge those of you who are in decision-making positions to carefully consider the meaning of NCCE's three-and-one-half year effort in Harlem Park. It was the hope and goal of the "With and For Parents" staff that through hands-on experience, not rhetoric, we could influence the outlook and actions of those who are in a position to involve low-income minority parents in the education of their children.

The survival skills of these parents are impressive, so is their potential to help their children. Since the public schools often represent the last, best hope for low-income children and families to improve their lives, it is a particular mission of NCCE to find ways to move parent involvement to new levels of influence. Here, in highly abbreviated form, are some lessons we feel others should know, understand and carefully consider as they formulate plans for new parent involvement efforts.

- Developing a working trust with parents cannot be put on a fast track—count on two years.

- The living and surviving conditions of urban families are far worse than most people know or understand, even those who have worked in cities before. If you have not spent a great deal of time in a low-income urban area lately, you don't know the conditions.

- Education and the improvement of student achievement through increased parent involvement is too narrow a focus for the low-income minority family. A broad view of the major assaults on daily living is required.

- This kind of project should begin earlier than sixth grade, before children have established a pattern of failure and low achievement. A great deal has changed since 1985 when we first designed the project. At that time, NCCE was unable to find support for beginning at the elementary school level. The Prudential Foundation was ahead of its time in agreeing to fund a dropout prevention project at the middle school level.

- The stereotype of low-income parents as having no potential or interest in helping their children is not true. Raising the self-confidence of low-income minority parents to become involved in schools on behalf of their children is an achievable goal. There are techniques, materials and approaches that pay off.

- A project of this kind should operate for a minimum of five years in order to obtain a more adequate test of materials and ideas.

- Parent involvement approaches need to be rethought and restructured as extensively as schools and school systems.

- One or more male staff members is essential in such a project. If you cannot find any with the needed experience, train them. The importance of their presence to both boys and girls cannot be overemphasized.

- Face squarely the years-later consequences for parents of current middle schoolers who had children when they themselves were middle school age. Approaches and materials that build respect and self-confidence are vital to enable these young parents to succeed in such a project.

- The pervasiveness of drugs in this neighborhood had a devastating effect on the sense of community. Many of the residents had a bunker mentality. We believe similar weakening and fragmentation of neighborhood bonds will be encountered in other low-income urban neighborhoods.

- As important as it is to pay intensive attention to parents, excluding their children from the project is a mistake. Children must be involved simultaneously at some level or parents will not be as well engaged. The inclusion of children is a key ingredient in parent involvement.

- Conventional research and evaluation procedures should be reconsidered or abandoned in favor of measures that account for the severity of the issues confronted. The danger with using conventional measures is that conclusions may be drawn that the project failed or fell far short of its goals because signs of success like increased staying power in a neighborhood or school are overlooked.

William Rioux designed the "With and For Parents" project and was its first director. He is currently executive director of the National Committee for Citizens in Education.

Index

The entire text of this book is about the "With and For Parents" dropout prevention program in the Harlem Park neighborhood of Baltimore, Maryland. Look under specific headings for additional information relating to the program in Harlem Park.